BUYER PERSONAS

BUYER
PERSONAS

JIM KRAUS AND ADELE REVELLA

BUYER PERSONAS

REVISED AND EXPANDED

GAIN DEEP INSIGHT INTO
YOUR CUSTOMERS' BUYING DECISIONS
AND WIN MORE BUSINESS

WILEY

Published by John Wiley & Sons, Inc., Hoboken, New Jersey.
Published simultaneously in Canada.

For general information on our other products and services or for technical support, please contact our Customer Care Department within the United States at (800) 762-2974, outside the United States at (317) 572-3993 or fax (317) 572-4002.

Wiley also publishes its books in a variety of electronic formats. Some content that appears in print may not be available in electronic formats. For more information about Wiley products, visit our web site at www.wiley.com.

Library of Congress Cataloging-in-Publication Data is available:

ISBN 9781394236336 (cloth)
ISBN 9781394236343 (epub)
ISBN 9781394236350 (epdf)

COVER DESIGN: PAUL MCCARTHY
COVER IMAGE: © GETTY IMAGES | MICHAEL BLANN

SKY10076936_060624

This book is dedicated to every marketer who questions the wisdom of making stuff up.

Contents

BUYER PERSONAS

Introduction: Listen First, Then Speak

A lot has changed in the marketing world since the first edition of *Buyer Personas* was published in 2015.

- Digital marketing has continued its rise as the Internet, social media, and mobile technology are deeply embedded and interconnected in how we live our lives and how we look for solutions to meet our varied needs.
- Search engine optimization (SEO) has become more sophisticated as brands compete to capture their customers' attention and engage with them in more productive ways when they do.
- Marketers are increasingly using data to personalize their campaigns as advertising, product recommendations, and tailored content have all become more sophisticated.
- Companies are experimenting (and having success) with emerging approaches such as account-based marketing (ABM) and product-led growth (PLG).
- Generative AI (GenAI) is changing the way marketers develop ideas and create engaging content more quickly at scale.

- Throw in the rise of video marketing, user-generated content (UGC), interactive content, voice search optimization, and on and on – and well, you get the picture.

Undoubtedly, as some of these approaches gain traction and evolve, others will die off without demonstrable results, and new methods of engaging with prospective buyers will emerge. *The one thing that hasn't changed – or ever will – is the need for marketers to deeply understand what causes buyers to purchase your solution, a competitor's products, or nothing at all.* With this knowledge, marketers have everything they need to influence buyers and generate more revenue and profits for their organization. Without this knowledge, it's guessing and hoping for the best (not a great long-term strategy).

The purpose of this revised and expanded edition of *Buyer Personas* is to show you exactly how to take all the guesswork out of your marketing. Regardless of your strategy *du jour*, a Buyer Persona is the foundation of your marketing house from which you can erect the framing, hang the drywall, and add the plumbing and electricity. It will inform nearly every marketing and sales decision you make and provide you a distinct advantage because you will know the who, what, where, and why your prospective customers make the buying decisions that they do in a way that your competitors can't match.

Understanding Your Buyer's Story

"So, what brings you in here to see me?"

That question is spoken countless times every day in doctor's offices, car repair shops, bank loan offices, law firms, and hundreds of other professional establishments. What usually follows that question is the customer's narrative describing their problem.

- "My daughter is entering college next year and I want to explore loan options for her education."
- "It's probably nothing, doctor, but I've been wondering about a small change I've noticed recently . . ."

- "The engine has been making the strangest sound when I drive downhill. It all started right after I loaned the car to my brother-in-law, who said he used it to move his large collection of Civil War cannon balls."
- "I'm concerned that my cat has been pacing back and forth at night and making very loud howls."

Listening is an essential part of any first meeting. It's how professionals learn about their customers' concerns, goals, and expectations so that they can present a relevant solution.

Yet in many organizations this one-to-one communication between marketing professionals and their customers is infrequent – if it happens at all.

How often do you have an opportunity to listen to your customers describe their problems? Do you know how to ask the questions that will make this conversation valuable for you and your customer? And most important, do you know how to apply what you've heard to become a more effective marketer?

The art and science of asking probing questions and carefully listening to your customers' responses lie at the core of the Buyer Persona concept. It's the key to discovering their mindsets and the motivation that prompts them to purchase a solution like yours.

One marketing professional confessed to us after conducting their first buyer interview, "This is almost like cheating; like getting the exam paper weeks before the final. Instead of trying to guess what matters, I now know not only what the customer wants – I realize how they go about it."

This is the power of the Buyer Persona. Built around a story about your customers' buying decision, the Buyer Persona reveals insight into your buyer's expectations and concerns as they look for options, winnow down their choices, and make a decision.

This book will show you how you can listen to your buyers' stories to gain insight into the factors that trigger their search, how they define success, and what affects their final decision that a particular approach is the best one for them. We'll show you how the buyer's personal narrative reveals language and phrases that will resonate with other buyers with similar concerns and how to define and focus on the activities that compel buyers to take action. You will see how giving buyers the clearly articulated information they seek, in the language they understand, when and where they need it, is the essence of effective marketing.

More Than Just a Profile of Your Prospective Buyers

In the simplest terms, Buyer Personas are examples or archetypes of real buyers that allow marketers to craft strategies to promote products and services to the people who might buy them. During the past few decades, the term has almost become a marketing mantra.

But as this book will show, the growing interest in Buyer Personas has resulted in confusion about how they are created, how they are used, and their ultimate effectiveness.

It's the intention of this book to provide some much-needed clarity.

The marketer's need to understand their market is hardly new. But the depth of insight required is increasing exponentially as technological advances demand that organizations rethink how they sell everything from music and books to bulldozers and information technology. A client at one of the world's leading software firms described it this way: "What we are selling is changing; who we are selling to is changing (some are people we've never sold to before); and how these customers want to be engaged, marketed, and sold to is changing too."

Buyer Personas have a lot to do with attaining that kind of alignment, but not in the way that marketers often use them, which is basically to build a profile of the people who are their intended customers. Rather, the contention of this book is that when Buyer Personas evolve from authentic stories related by actual buyers – in the form of one-on-one interviews – the methodology and presentation allow you to capture the buyer's expectations and the factors that influence them. Then, and only then, can you truly stand in your buyers' shoes and consider the buying decision from the buyer's point of view. This goes way beyond buyer profiling, but most marketers don't realize that.

Not long ago, we met with executives from a large corporation who had spent hundreds of thousands of dollars for research on "Buyer Personas" that were essentially worthless. The company had purchased profiles about the people who buy, but these failed to capture the crucially important stories revealing how buyers make this type of decision. We've also seen companies purchase over-segmented research that defined dozens of Buyer Personas, a number that would be feasibly impossible for them to tailor their marketing with any effectiveness.

In both of these cases, the company had lost its way by focusing on the goal to build Buyer Personas without a clear plan to ensure that they contain useful findings.

Naturally, it's far easier to make educated guesses and assumptions about what buyers may be thinking based on extrapolations of your own knowledge or intuition. That's certainly how large aspects of the marketing community have functioned for decades. But the climate of social and technological change favors companies that embrace a culture of buyer understanding that allows them to adapt to customer needs. Just consider the major technology players that have receded or disappeared: AOL, Digital, Polaroid, Wang, AltaVista, Netscape, Fairchild Semiconductor, Palm, Sun Microsystems. The list could run for pages. Each of these companies was outrun by competitors who possessed greater clarity about their buyers' expectations.

Will This Approach Work for You?

This book is for marketing professionals who want to avoid that kind of dire scenario, whether they work in the business-to-business (B2B) or the business-to-consumer (B2C) arena. It is specifically aimed at marketers of "high-consideration" products, services, and solutions – buying decisions that require a considerable investment of your buyers' thought and time. Examples of high-consideration decisions range from selecting the right vendor of capital equipment, or picking which college to attend, to carefully choosing a new car, or the most appropriate location for office space. This decision-making process differs markedly from impulse purchases made in a grocery store or at the checkout register.

When you consider that we want to interview buyers to capture their story, it is easy to understand why a detailed narrative about a choice between new automobiles would be immensely useful. In contrast, little insight would be gained as a result of asking a buyer to explain why they decided to purchase a particular pack of gum.

Although the Internet and artificial intelligence (AI) more recently have given us instant access to immense knowledge, even the most sophisticated applications won't reveal what you can learn by listening to your buyer's stories. Just as there is nothing to acquaint you with a foreign culture as intimately as staying with a native family in their home, the best way to gain deep insight into your buyer's mindset is to spend quality time with them.

The Buyer Persona methodology outlined in this book will help companies avoid the consequences that inevitably engulf organizations that fail to listen intensely to their buyers. In the pages to come, we will explain how you can use Buyer Personas to craft successful marketing strategies based on insight that would otherwise be nearly impossible to acquire. We will show how this can be done without exorbitant investments in money, time, or labor. It just requires adhering to a well-defined process, mastering a few skills, and honing your analytical thinking. This is a craft and a set of skills that can be learned, and this book will serve as your primer for how you or your organization can achieve this.

How the Book Is Organized and What's New

We've organized the book into four parts.

In Part I, you'll learn what a Buyer Persona is, and what it is not. You'll find out why so many Buyer Personas are not as useful as they should be, and what you need to do to ensure the success of your Buyer Persona initiative. In this updated edition, you'll also get an inside look at how one of the authors chose a vacation destination that demonstrates the importance of understanding the buying decision and why it should be the cornerstone of your Buyer Persona.

In Part II, we'll get into the nitty-gritty of how to find, recruit, and conduct buyer interviews so they reveal everything you need to know to develop your Buyer Persona. We've added an entirely new chapter that provides detailed guidance about how to design and set up your Buyer Persona study for success. We'll also introduce you to a Buyer Persona we developed (for magnetic resonance imaging [MRI] machines) and use it throughout the book so you can see how one step in a persona study leads to the next.

Part III focuses on mining your interviews for Buying Insights and creating Buyer Personas that will be easily understood and widely leveraged across your organization. We've also added a new chapter on conducting survey research to enhance the Buying Insights from your persona.

Finally, in Part IV, we'll share step-by-step guidance about how to use Buyer Personas to define your marketing strategies. You'll learn how to rely on Buyer Persona insights to develop your messaging and marketing activities to align with your sales organization, and in the final chapter, we'll recommend a place to begin and explain our vision for the future role of Buyer Personas.

We are excited that you share our interest in Buyer Personas and hope that this updated and expanded version of the book will help you join the growing ranks of buyer-expert marketers.

PART

I

The Art and Science
of Buyer Personas

Ask someone in marketing what a "Buyer Persona" is and more likely than not they are going to say something such as:

- "It's a fictional archetype of a *functional role* or *title* including their interests, values, challenges, and priorities."
- "It's a profile of a *person* including demographics such as age, gender, income, occupation, and location."
- "It's a detailed description of *someone* who represents your target audience or ideal customer."

These answers aren't terribly surprising given that virtually anyone associated with the craft of marketing has written, spoken, or referenced Buyer Personas in exactly such a way over the past 20–30 years. And we know that there are literally hundreds of organizations (probably thousands!) that have developed "Buyer Personas" just like this to attract and win more business.

Unfortunately, many of these organizations have also come to realize that this type of *audience-based* Buyer Persona – one that profiles an *individual* or *role* – **provides little to no insight into what influences**

a prospective customer's buying decision. This type of persona may give you a general sense of a particular role involved in the buying decision – who they are and what they care about in broad terms – but it omits critical insights that marketers need to help their organizations attract and convert more business, including:

- What triggers a prospective buyer to start looking for a particular solution that you offer in the first place?
- What specific outcomes do buyers expect from making an investment in this solution?
- What fears, concerns, and trepidations do buyers have about making this investment, or making it with you?
- What questions will buyers ask as they figure out what providers and solutions to consider, winnow down their choices, and make a final decision?
- What are the key steps in the buyer's journey? Who is involved in the process? What information sources do they use and trust?

Organizations that rely on profiles of different individuals or roles involved in the buying decision often end up developing too many personas that overcomplicate their strategies and messaging and fail to connect with buyers in ways that inspire trust and make them confident in their buying decisions.

Fortunately, there is better way, and we'll spend the majority of this book describing exactly how to develop Buyer Personas that reveal deep insight into the who, what, where, and why buyers make the buying decisions that they do. This type of *buying decision-based persona* will take all the guesswork out of your marketing activities so the wind is continuously at your back as you strive to deeply connect with buyers.

In this first part of the book, we are going to focus on three foundational elements of a Buyer Persona:

- Why a Buyer Persona based on insights into the buying decision is vastly superior to a profile of an individual or role that may be involved in it.

- The five types of Buying Insight you need for your Buyer Persona and why each is important.
- Why one-on-one interviews with buyers are by far the best way to create your Buyer Personas.

Once we've established these core tenets, the rest of the book will get into the nitty-gritty of how you can develop Buyer Personas that will become the definitive source for what your prospective buyers need to know and experience to make a confident buying decision about a solution that you offer. These Buyer Personas create alignment across the organization and will quickly become the unifying "voice of the buyer" that points everyone in the optimal direction.

1 | Understanding Buying Decisions and the People Who Make Them

In some marketing courses and websites, Buyer Personas are defined as something similar to Figure 1.1.

Here we see John, a fictional archetype who is meant to represent a typical Operations Manager. The graphic outline gives us information about John's education, age, to whom he reports, his skills, the incentives and rewards from his job (keeping his job and an occasional raise), and how he spends his free time (family, church, a weekly poker game with his friends); plus, how he stays current on the latest trends in his industry, broken down into four categories. This is a Buyer Profile that is heavy on data that could be readily gleaned from online research, social media, artificial intelligence (AI), and other sources.

The Buyer Profile has gained a lot of traction because it is a useful tool to help you think about your target buyers as real people, with actual families, typical bosses, and human concerns. For the same reason

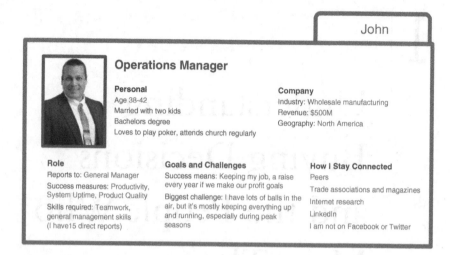

Figure 1.1   Example Buyer Profile.

that we find it far easier to communicate via social media when we have a photograph of a person we have never met in person, the Buyer Profile creates a sense of the human connection with people whom we have never met face-to-face. If you've ever built a relationship with someone through social media, you may have noticed that your first in-person encounter feels a lot like running into an old friend. The photograph and details of this person's job or personal life have likely shaped your interactions and created a sense of intimacy despite the fact that you live and work in very different circumstances.

Where Buyer Profiles Fall Short

While a Buyer Profile has value for marketers – and it should be *part* of your Buyer Persona – it tells us nothing about how buyers make a buying decision. We see John reads industry publications, belongs to industry trade groups, and uses the Internet when searching for solutions. Alas, the same could be said for about 99% of other business professionals working at a comparable managerial level.

Let's say John is looking for a new logistics management supplier. From this template, what do we know about what's motivating John to find a new supplier? What does he expect to be different once he makes this switch? What is very important to John about the appearance of the packaging and enclosures in the shipments sent to retailers? What does John dislike about a lot of the providers he has used in the past?

Marketers hoping to interest John in their logistics services using just his Buyer Profile template won't find much useful intelligence here. Instead, they would need to use this profile to imagine (guess?) how John would respond to their messaging when sitting at his desk.

It's difficult to imagine how this approach to Buyer Personas will help marketers of logistics solutions know what they need to do to help John see their solution as a perfect fit for his needs. Further, it is unlikely that this company's marketers will use this tool to persuade their internal stakeholders that a different approach to their messaging and marketing activities will set their merchandise or services apart from their competition.

Buyer Profiles will not transform this marketer's ability to think like John. But suppose you knew what John is looking for when he is considering signing a contract with a new provider, why he has been dissatisfied with other providers in the past, and a score of other specific details about how John makes his decision. And suppose that these actionable details are things that neither you, nor your own salespeople, nor the competition has ever heard before. These are the types of *Buying Insights* that will give you clear guidance for the decisions you need to make to win John's business.

What a Family Vacation Can Teach Us About the Buying Decision

For the remainder of this chapter, we are going to take you through a first-person account of an actual buying decision I recently went through. Doing so will:

- Show you why it's so important for marketers to understand the mindset and steps that buyers take when making a buying decision, and
- Introduce you to the types of Buying Insights that should be part of your Buyer Persona.

Some Background

Every year, my extended family and I go on vacation together. Everyone goes – spouses, kids, aunts, uncles, cousins, grandparents. I think someone even brought their pet turtle one year. Point is, there's a lot of us and it's a trip everyone looks forward to and plans their schedules around. We always have a great time and return home relaxed, refreshed, and grateful for the time together.

To keep things interesting, we pick a different location each year and one member of the family is randomly chosen as the "Squad Leader" for that trip. He or she chooses the destination, a place to stay, and some fun activities we can all do together. Once we get back from a trip, planning for the next one starts shortly after.

Such was the case early last year when we had just returned from one of these trips and it was time to randomly select the Squad Leader for our next adventure. I won't divulge the scientific way we do this, but there's a hat and pieces of paper involved.

Now, I can't speak for other members of my family, but my thinking at that exact moment went something like this:

- *Super – we had such a great time on the last trip, I can't wait to see where we go next!*
- *I hope we go to Europe, or maybe some place more tropical, or even a part of the U.S. where we've never been.*
- *Maybe we can try Yellowstone, Zion or one of the other National Parks. We've never done that before.*
- *Please, oh please, oh please, don't pick me as the Squad Leader!*

I think I make reasonably good decisions most of the time, but organizing a trip like this for so many people is not exactly in my wheelhouse, particularly when our past trips have been so successful. And, since I've perfected my role as a benign and supportive attendee, I didn't see any reason to mess with leadership responsibilities now.

By my telling this story, you can probably guess that my name *did* come out of that hat, which meant I needed to start planning for our next trip right away. I figured my chances of pulling this off were at least fifty-fifty. I mean, if humankind can put a person on the moon, split the atom, and raise pyramids from the sand, I can certainly plan a week's vacation for one eager, if not occasionally judgmental family!

My Mindset

Since every Squad Leader needs a clear set of objectives, I started thinking about what I wanted out of this trip. I envisioned new adventures where everyone had a great time and experienced a few things they had never done before. I pictured a lot of family-time together, talking, laughing, and catching up on each other's lives. I also wanted everyone to have a chance to relax and recharge from the day-to-day pressures of life.

These were broad aspirations, and I was a bit anxious, so I took a minute to jot down a few specific requirements that I thought would help me focus – see Figure 1.2.

The Initial Search

To reduce the initial ocean of possibilities, I decided to focus on warm, tropical locations. We had been to a colder climate on our last trip, so a warmer venue would be a welcome change. And, since we roughed it a bit last time – camping, hiking, kayaking – I decided to focus on resort hotels where we could all relax at a more leisurely pace and enjoy some of the finer amenities that these destinations offer.

Family Vacation Requirements

- Nice weather
- Beautiful destination in a safe environment
- Clean accommodations with modern amenities
- Fun activities and new adventures
- Downtime to relax and do nothing
- Good, local cuisine
- Great guest service - friendly, attentive, helpful
- Reasonable price that's within our budget

Figure 1.2   Family vacation requirements.

From there, I asked for advice from friends and did a little online research – mainly visiting different travel and resort websites. The websites gave me an initial feel for what each resort offered, including rooms, dining options, beachfront property, pools, activities, excursions, and spa facilities. I also got a preliminary sense of price for each one.

Based on these inputs, I narrowed it down to three resorts that had the main things I was looking for and were within the budget range my family had agreed upon.

On a scale of 1 (panicked) to 10 (very confident), my comfort level was about 3 at that point. I realize that's a low level of confidence, but this is an important trip for my family, and I didn't want to be THE ONE to mess it up!

Evaluating Options

My next step was to dig in and investigate each resort more closely. I never expressly stated this to anyone (maybe not even myself!), but my two overarching questions at that point were:

- Which resort has the best chance of providing us with all the things *we* want?
- Which resort has the least likelihood of failing *me* in some way?

The first question was impersonal and objective. All I needed to do was investigate the resorts one-by-one to see what each of them offered and make my assessment.

The second question was highly personal. I needed to eliminate any chance of something falling short of expectations (that I would be blamed for!). Things like dirty rooms, bad service, poor food quality, and unanticipated expenses were all top of mind.

With those two questions lurking in my mind, I moved to the next phase of my search where I visited each resort's website again, read more online reviews from prior guests, and contacted each hotel directly to get more information and ask questions.

Here's a summary of my experience with each of the three resorts that I'll call *Coconut Palms*, *Coral Breeze*, and *Lagoon Oasis* (all pseudonyms).

Coconut Palms   The Coconut Palms website had a few stock images of pools, restaurants, and outdoor activities in a resort setting – none were of the *actual* resort itself.

I found a handful of online reviews that ranged from very negative to somewhat positive. No one gave glowing marks. When a prior guest gave a negative review, the resort did not apologize, offer an explanation, or even seek additional information. In fact, there was no reply at all.

When I called the resort directly, it went to voicemail. Someone did call me back a few minutes later, but they weren't able to answer several basic questions I had about their rooms and dining options.

Coral Breeze   Coral Breeze's website had beautiful photos of the actual resort including the rooms, restaurants, pools, beaches, golf course, and the spa. It even had a panoramic video of their entire property that I could zoom in and out of.

Online reviews were plentiful and included mostly positive ratings along with a few negative comments that Coral Breeze addressed by responding to each reviewer quickly and directly.

When I called the resort, someone picked up immediately and patiently answered most of the questions I had.

Lagoon Oasis   Like Coral Breeze, I had a similarly good experience with Lagoon Oasis in terms of the quality of their website, photos, videos, and online reviews. Their website also had a simple, one-page overview of the key features and amenities of their hotel compared to other resorts in the area, including Coconut Palms and Coral Breeze.

When I called Lagoon Oasis directly, I was quickly routed to a Guest Relations Representative ("Rep") who:

- Asked me how many people were in my party, the purpose of our trip, the types of activities we enjoy, and what a "perfect vacation" might look like for us.
- Answered all my questions patiently along with his personal suggestions about the activities he thought we would enjoy based on our preferences.

- Arranged a time to call me back later in the day so he could give me more specific recommendations and details about the rooms, restaurants, activities, and excursions that were tailored to everything we spoke about.
- Left his direct number in case I had any additional questions.
- Offered to book the entire vacation for me if we decided to stay with them or alternatively book online if I preferred.

The Decision

After all of this, I ultimately chose Lagoon Oasis. I suspect, you would too. Unless you're a member of my family, my choosing Lagoon Oasis isn't important. But, for marketers trying to influence prospective buyers, understanding WHY I chose Lagoon Oasis is important. Let's dig into this a bit more, as Lagoon Oasis understood several things better than the other resorts I was considering.

First, Lagoon Oasis recognized that this was a *high-consideration buying decision* for me – not life or death, but these vacations are important to my family and there is a keen interest in making them as enjoyable as possible for everyone. I wasn't going to just pick a resort willy-nilly. I needed to take some time and really investigate my options.

Second, they realized that I didn't want to disappoint my family *by making a bad choice*. I was actually more fearful of making the "wrong" choice than I was excited about making the "right" one. High-consideration buying decisions are often like that. You want the upside benefits, but you also want to minimize the risks that something could go wrong or fall short of expectations.

Third, Lagoon Oasis understood that although I was the person they were interacting with, there were *multiple people influencing the buying decision* – my entire family in this case. My needs and preferences were important (got to take care of #1, right!), but my entire family was going to be impacted by this decision and they were on my mind throughout the process.

Finally, Lagoon Oasis recognized that I was going to consider other resorts and *comparing my options would be difficult*. They were right. I never searched for a resort before. I never stayed at the ones I was considering. And, on the surface, they all seemed pretty similar. Trying to compare them was difficult and stressful.

Looking across these factors, what Lagoon Oasis really understood better than the others is this fundamental buying truth:

> The organization that does the best job of making a buyer feel CONFIDENT and SECURE in their buying decision usually wins the business.

How Lagoon Oasis Earned My Business

So, what did Lagoon Oasis actually say and do to make me confident in choosing them? And where did Coconut Palms and Coral Breeze miss the mark in comparison?

It's useful to examine this at both the early and later stages of my buying journey.

In the **EARLY** stages:

Lagoon Oasis recognized that I'd do some of my own research before contacting them to figure out what their resort looked like, what they offered, and what prior guests were saying. To meet my buying needs at this early stage, they provided photos and videos on their website of everything on and around their property. By the sheer number and quality of online reviews, I could tell that past guests went out of their way to share their great experiences. By directly responding to the few negative reviews they received, Lagoon Oasis also showed me that they cared about the guest experience. As a result, my confidence and sense of security to trust Lagoon Oasis with our vacation took root.

Coral Breeze also gave me some confidence early on. Like Lagoon Oasis, their website had lots of appealing photos of the property, they offered a wide variety of activities, and most of the online reviews were positive. Although Lagoon Oasis had an edge, Coral Breeze was still in the running at this early stage.

Although I did end up contacting Coconut Palms, they fell out of consideration almost immediately. A poor website with only stock photos told me they weren't proud of their property (and that they might even be hiding something!). Poor guest reviews reinforced my uneasiness to trust them.

In the **LATER** stages of my buying journey:

Lagoon Oasis took the time to ask what a "perfect vacation" looked like for my family and kept asking me questions to ensure that any lingering concerns I had were fully addressed. I didn't need to guess or hope they would – Lagoon Oasis SHOWED me by providing the information and details I needed to feel confident on my own. They even suggested activities we should skip and provided a buying experience that made it easy to book with them. Most importantly, once they understood what I wanted, it became less about everything THEY offered and more about how their resort could best meet MY family's needs. Consequently, my confidence and sense of security choosing Lagoon Oasis grew rapidly and it's *the* reason that I ultimately chose them.

My interactions with Coral Breeze were also good – they were friendly, attentive, and helpful overall. But unlike Lagoon Oasis, they didn't take the time to really understand my family's interests and preferences, or address some of the questions I had. I also didn't get a clear vision of how Coral Breeze would meet our specific needs – we'd have to figure some of that out on our own. Consequently, they seemed like a riskier option, so I didn't choose them.

Focus Your Buyer Personas on the Buying Decision

At this point, you may be asking yourself, so what? There's some nice lessons in this story that most marketers can relate to, but what's the point in the context of Buyer Personas – both the title and focus of this book?

The point is, rather than assuming or accepting the notion that a Buyer Persona is simply a fictional avatar of an individual or role involved in the buying decision — the more traditional, but limiting view of what a Buyer Persona is — Lagoon Oasis stopped and asked themselves: ***what Buying Insights do we need that will enable us to better influence prospective buyers and give them the confidence they need to choose us?*** Let's take a minute and really think about that question. Put yourself in the shoes of someone in Lagoon Oasis's marketing department and ask yourself, what types of insights would you need to have to develop strategies, messaging, and experiences that:

- Increase buyer awareness of the resort,
- Drive consideration once prospective buyers become aware of the resort, and
- Convert more business as prospective buyers weigh their options and make a choice.

Lagoon Oasis didn't settle, and neither should you. Think about insights that you would need to eliminate all the guesswork in marketing, allowing you to focus on strategies that break through the clutter and have the desired effect on the buying decision.

If you answered the question honestly, you'd acknowledge that knowing a few things about me as an individual isn't going to help that much. Clayton Christensen, the renowned academic, consultant, and author of *The Innovator's Dilemma*, once said:

> I'm 6-feet-8-inches tall. My shoe size is 16. My wife and I have sent all our children off to college. I live in a suburb of Boston and drive a Honda minivan to work. I have a lot of other characteristics and attributes. But these characteristics have not yet caused me to go out and buy *The New York Times* today. There might be a correlation between some of these characteristics and the propensity of customers to purchase the Times. But those attributes don't cause me to buy that paper — or any product.

Point taken! Rather than a profile of an individual or role in the buying decision, what you really need is ***insight into the <u>buying decision</u>***

they are making. Let's consider three things that Lagoon Oasis understood about the buying decision I was making and how they used that knowledge to win my business. In Chapter 2, we'll use these observations to create a framework for Buyer Personas that will inform nearly every marketing and sales decision you make (teaser alert!)

High-consideration Buying Decisions

The first thing Lagoon Oasis realized is that searching for and selecting a resort destination is a *high-consideration buying decision*. A high-consideration decision means:

- Prospective buyers consider multiple options to fulfill their needs.
- Buyers haven't made this decision before or have done so infrequently.
- Multiple individuals are involved in the decision directly or indirectly.
- There is a lot at stake for the individuals and organizations (if B2B) involved in the buying decision.

Since this was a high-consideration buying decision, Lagoon Oasis knew I'd be anxious about making the best choice possible and that I'd need certain things to feel confident, including lots of details about the resort, expert guidance during my buying journey, and evidence that Lagoon Oasis cared about my family's needs and could fulfill them.

If you look back at all the things Lagoon Oasis did throughout my buying journey, you'll see that they understood all of this and delivered the information and evaluation experience I needed.

Multiple Stages in the Buying Journey

Lagoon Oasis also recognized that my buying needs would evolve as I got deeper into my search and that I'd want different types of information and interactions with them as things progressed.

Early on, I didn't want a lot of information about each resort because it made me more anxious and confused. All I needed was enough information to help me decide who I was going to initially consider. Website photos of the resorts and online reviews from prior guests were the right amount of information to make that judgment.

Later in my buying journey, when I started to evaluate my options more closely, I was ready for the details. Now I wanted to see *exactly* how each resort was going to deliver the experience we wanted. It was at that point that Lagoon Oasis took time to understand my family's important needs and showed me exactly how they'd meet them. They also listened to my concerns and fully addressed each one. Consequently, my confidence in Lagoon Oasis grew.

Types of Buying Insights Needed

Lagoon Oasis also realized that they needed five different types of Buying Insights to develop strategies that would resonate with me throughout my buying journey, including:

1. **What caused me to start looking for a resort destination in the first place?** It was clear that Lagoon Oasis had done their homework and knew there were certain buyers, like me, that would be looking for a destination that catered to large families. Consequently, their website had lots of photos of families relaxing together and participating in fun activities and excursions. Later on, their Guest Relations Rep asked me about the purpose of our trip. Once I told him, he recommended activities and property features that were geared toward a large family vacation and all the experiences we wanted to have. At that moment, my perception of Lagoon Oasis went from a nameless resort – no better or worse than any of the others – to an actual place where my family and I could have a great time.

2. **What were the most important outcomes and experiences we wanted from the trip?** We sought new adventures, a lot of family time, and a chance to relax and recharge. Lagoon Oasis's website, online reviews, and my interactions with Guest Relations showed me that we'd get all of these things by staying with them.

The images on their website were enticing and included photos and information about zip-lining, four-wheeling, and snorkeling – all things we were interested in. Online reviews backed up the promise that these activities were both fun and safe. The Guest Relations Rep recommended which activities made the most sense for us and when to schedule them throughout our stay. By interspersing these activities with sufficient downtime in between, I knew we'd also have plenty of time to relax. After all of these interactions, did I feel confident that we'd get the outcomes we wanted? You bet!

3. **What worries did I have about something going wrong or not meeting expectations?** I had four primary concerns, and Lagoon Oasis alleviated each of them:

   - **Dirty rooms:** Photos of pristine rooms and glowing guest reviews eliminated any trepidations I had about cleanliness.
   - **Bad service:** The Guest Relations Rep was knowledgeable, attentive, and responsive. Prior guests went out of their way to write positive reviews about specific members of the resort staff. I was confident the service would be top-notch.
   - **Poor food quality:** Diverse restaurant options available inside and outside of the resort, along with beautiful images of delicious food and positive guest reviews, squashed any concerns I had.
   - **Higher costs than anticipated:** Costs for accommodations, transport to and from the resort, activities, excursions, and food were all included, itemized, and transparent. Guest Relations took time to review all of them with me so I was confident that no hidden expenses would pop up unexpectedly.

4. **What were the requirements I'd use to evaluate my options and make a decision?** Recall that early on, I jotted down eight things on a piece of paper that I was looking for – nice weather, safe environment, clean accommodations, modern amenities, etc. I went back to these notes several times as I investigated each of

the three resorts. It kept me on track and enabled me to make a thorough and objective decision. Coconut Palms and Coral Breeze addressed some of these requirements. Lagoon Oasis fulfilled all of them.

5. **What did my buying journey look like – steps taken, resources used, and people involved?** Lagoon Oasis clearly understood the major steps I'd take during the time I searched for resort options, weighed the pros and cons of each property, and made a final decision. They knew their website and guest reviews would be critical touchpoints early on if I was going to initially consider them. Once I dug into a few of the resorts more closely, Lagoon Oasis shrewdly leveraged their Guest Relations Reps as the primary means for educating me about everything their resort had to offer and aligning that with my family's needs and preferences. They also made it easy for me to compare what they had to offer versus other options I was considering (recall the comparison information they made available on their website).

Taken together, these five Buying Insights gave Lagoon Oasis everything they needed to provide me with the right type and amount of information, in the right way, at the right time. As a result, they earned my trust and differentiated themselves from the other options I was considering.

Next Steps

We've had a chance to consider the types of Buying Insights that marketers need to influence prospective buyers. When it comes to high-consideration buying decisions, a Buyer Persona that only provides descriptive characteristics of a particular individual or role is not enough. We can do better!

However, there is still one important buying predicament that we need to address directly to ensure that our Buyer Personas are as valuable as they can be to BOTH marketing and sales. That is, what happens when a prospective buyer starts looking for a solution to a need that they have, expresses interest in buying it, but then does nothing? They stick with the status quo. Talk to any salesperson and they will tell you that "customer inaction" is one of the toughest challenges they face, particularly considering how much time and energy is expended getting buyers to the precipice of making a buying decision. An impactful Buyer Persona will help them overcome this challenge and, in doing so, elevate the value of marketing.

In the next chapter we'll examine some compelling new evidence that shows why understanding the buying decision is critical to helping sales professionals overcome *customer inaction*. Then we'll lay out a logical framework for Buyer Personas that will provide you with the Buying Insights you need to influence buyers, so they choose you rather than your competitors or the status quo. Hundreds of companies and thousands of marketers have used this exact same approach to take all the guesswork out of their marketing and sales activities – you can too!

Summary

In this chapter, we covered the following points:

- High-consideration buying decisions typically involve multiple decision influencers, a competitive search and evaluation process, and some level of risk.
- These can be business-to-consumer (B2C) buying decisions, such as the resort example, or business-to-business (B2B), such as buying enterprise software, a piece of equipment, or engaging in a professional services contract.
- Buyers are often anxious – they have likely never made this type of buying decision before, or only infrequently, and there is confusion about the different options available.

- Consequently, whoever does the best job of making a buyer feel confident and secure in their buying decision usually wins the business.
- To do this, you need more than just a Buyer Profile (a fictional archetype of an individual or role involved in the buying decision). You need insight into why and how prospective buyers make the buying decisions that they do. Only then can you align with a buyer's needs and differentiate yourself throughout their buying journey.
- A Buyer Persona reveals everything a prospective buyer wants to know and experience before they buy from you and will inform nearly every marketing and sales decision that you make.

2

Focus on Insights That Guide Marketing and Sales Enablement

In a simpler world, marketers would only need to worry about influencing one type of buyer – those that have already made up their mind that they are going to buy something. These are buyers that are committed to moving away from the status quo, so marketers need not worry about convincing them that their solution is better than what they are doing now.

Alas, this simpler world does not exist. Talk to any sales professional and they will tell you that overcoming *customer inaction* – a prospective buyer's decision not to purchase anything, even after going through the entire sales process and expressing purchase intent – is one of the biggest hurdles they face. By some estimates, 40–60% of deals today end up stalled in "no decision" purgatory. Countless hours and effort are spent trying to nudge, coax, and convince interested buyers to sign on the dotted line. This is a constant challenge for sales, but particularly when economic waters are choppy and there is a lot at stake for customers who don't want to buy anything that doesn't add assured value to their lives and businesses. For these buyers, it's not just about picking the "best" solution, it's about making a decision to buy anything at all versus sticking with the relative safety of the status quo.

For marketers, this is an opportunity to help sellers break the decision stalemate with their anxious buyers. By understanding and anticipating the outcomes that prospective buyers need from their investment, and the questions and concerns they will have, marketing can provide sales with the tools they need to overcome *customer inaction* and close more business.

A Unique Opportunity

In their revealing book, *The JOLT Effect: How High Performers Overcome Customer Indecision,* Matthew Dixon and Ted McKenna partnered with dozens of companies across a variety of industries to collect and analyze more than 2.5 million sales calls. This unique, first-of-its-kind opportunity came about only because, as the world went on lockdown in the spring of 2020 due to COVID-19, conversations between sales and prospective buyers previously conducted in a customer's office started to take place on platforms such as Zoom, Teams, Webex, and others, where they could be recorded. By transcribing and digitizing these discussions, machine learning algorithms could be leveraged to organize and analyze all of this unstructured data. Dixon and McKenna's analysis revealed compelling new insights for anyone whose job it is to understand what causes *customer inaction* and how to overcome it. Only by digging into what they learned can we comprehend why it's so important to understand the buying decision and define a framework for Buyer Personas that provides the Buying Insights marketers need to help sales be more successful.

Why Interested Buyers Don't Buy

With data from millions of in-the-moment, unfiltered conversations between prospective buyers and sellers, Dixon and McKenna were able to tag all the deals where *customer inaction* occurred to figure out why so many otherwise interested buyers chose not to buy and stick with what they were already doing. Prior to their analysis, *customer inaction* was historically attributed to one cause: a customer's *preference for the status quo.* In other words, it was believed that when a customer chooses not to buy anything, it's because they think what they're already doing is better than buying something new or different. Sales training has long focused on helping sellers overcome this obstacle, instructing them to "relitigate" the sale by re-emphasizing the benefits of their solution and what the customer will miss out on if they don't buy. In other words, ratchet up the fear, uncertainty, and doubt (FUD).

In an ah-ha moment, the analysis showed that this is frequently a flawed strategy and actually detrimental to closing deals. Rather than continuing to push the benefits of buying their solution – and what buyers will miss out on if they don't – the most effective sellers anticipate and understand the fears that buyers have and take actions to navigate through them, particularly at the later stages of the buying journey. Instead of pressuring buyers, these sellers add clarity, calmness, and a steady hand to the proceedings. They realize that when buyers are ready to buy but still anxious, what they need most is confident assurance that things will work out.

By examining a few of the most compelling statistics from the study, we can begin to understand the magnitude and the importance of this revelation and the opportunity it affords marketing to help sales overcome *customer inaction.*

- First, Dixon and McKenna determined that the primary reason for a customer's inaction is more often caused by their inability to make a decision than a preference for the status quo – see Figure 2.1.

  This is a critical distinction, as *preference for the status quo* is a purposeful decision made by a buyer who has evaluated their options and determined that what they are doing now is better than any of the alternatives. In comparison, the *inability to make a decision* is passive and rooted in a buyer's fears. They haven't

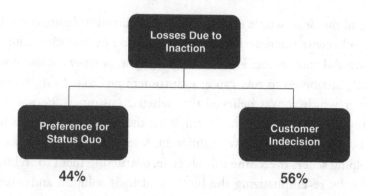

Figure 2.1   Breakdown of losses to inaction by root cause.

decided the status quo is better; they simply can't make up their mind, so they do nothing.

■ Even more insidious, the study found that a staggering 87% of all sales conversations have moderate-to-high levels of buyer indecision regardless of the sales outcome.

■ By examining deal outcomes, the study also showed that win rates drop precipitously as the level of buyer indecision grows – win rates are 45–55% when there are low rates of buyer indecision and drop below 5% when indecision is high.

In other words, **buyer indecision is everywhere, and it has a profound negative impact on sales!**

So why is there so much buyer indecision? Why do buyers have such a hard time moving away from the status quo, even when they've carefully examined their options and expressed interest in buying?

Pointing to decades of social science research, Dixon and McKenna correctly point out that buyer indecision is driven by their fear of messing up (error of commission) more so than missing out (error of omission):

But once they [buyers] have agreed that they should move on from the status quo, the thing they now fear – and fear more – is the failure that may result from their actions: what will happen not if they do nothing but rather if they do something. And those costs will be concrete and directly attributable to their decisions.

In other words, making the decision to buy something that falls short of expectations is a more significant risk to buyers because it is a concrete and observable action that can hurt their reputation. Conversely, not buying is a more passive, under-the-radar act. It is also much harder to personally blame one person for doing nothing – everyone is culpable.

So, if buyer indecision is everywhere, and it has such a negative impact on sales success, how do marketers help sellers and their organizations overcome it? Again, the Dixon and McKenna study provides some compelling guidance.

What the Best Sellers Do to Overcome Buyer Indecision

For decades, salespeople have been taught that when a prospective customer gets cold feet, they should emphasize everything the buyer will miss out on by sticking with the status quo. Instead, the opposite is true – rather than building a buyer's confidence and security, these approaches just make prospective customers more anxious and paralyze their ability to make a decision. In another startling finding, the Dixon and McKenna study showed that "relitigating" the sale with buyers actually hurts win rates 84% of the time! These tactics not only don't help – they actually hurt a seller's chances of closing the business – see Figure 2.2.

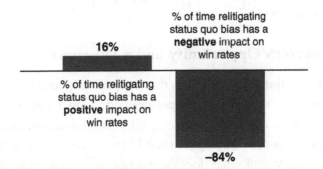

Figure 2.2   Impact of relitigating the status quo with indecisive buyers.

The reason for this is simple. At a certain point in their buying journey, interested buyers believe that the outcomes they can achieve are worthwhile. What they don't yet believe is that nothing will go wrong or fall short of expectations. Continuing to ratchet up the "fear of missing out" (FOMO) feels like high-pressure sales tactics, rather than providing buyers with what they need to feel confident and secure moving away from the status quo. As Dixon and McKenna put it:

> Our research shows that the best sellers have figured out that there is a point in the sale where their job is no longer convincing the customer how they'll succeed by making the purchase; it's about proving to the customer that they won't fail by making the purchase.

The study revealed that instead of high-pressure sales tactics, the most effective sellers overcome buyer indecision by:

- Establishing themselves as subject-matter experts that navigate buyers through their buying journey.
- Anticipating buyer needs and addressing unstated concerns.
- Limiting the litany of information coming at buyers so they focus only on what is most important relative to their desired outcomes.

These sellers use their acute understanding of a buyer's mindset at the early and later stages of the buying journey to bolster their confidence that they will be successful.

The Marketer's Opportunity and a Dilemma

This is all well and good for sellers that have the opportunity to interact with buyers on a regular basis. These sellers develop a sixth sense about a buyer's needs, goals, and concerns as they spend time interacting with them throughout their buying journey. They can test different strategies, learn what works and what doesn't, and fine-tune their approach to be more successful.

But what about the marketer who rarely has the opportunity to talk to prospective customers and is being asked to develop strategies that influence an *entire market of buyers*, not just one buyer at a time? What about the marketer that is simultaneously being asked to drive more leads and help sellers convert more business across what we now understand are three unique buying situations?

Buying Situation 1: Choosing the Best Option (No Customer Inaction Present)

This is when buyers are committed to buying something and they weigh the pros and cons of different options to decide which will achieve the outcomes that they seek and minimize the risk that something will go wrong. The resort vacation example in Chapter 1 is a good example of this type of buying situation. On these occasions, *marketers are trying to help their organizations "make the case" that they are the best option from the alternatives buyers are considering.*

Buying Situation 2: Inability to Make a Decision

This is when buyers are interested in buying something, but they are anxious and indecisive. They're nervous something could go wrong, or they won't make the "best" decision from the options they're considering. As a result, they are paralyzed and stick with the status quo because it's considered the least risky option. These are lose–lose situations because buyers don't make a purchase that helps them and their organizations (if business-to-business [B2B]), sellers don't close the business, and a significant amount of time and resources are wasted on both sides. On these occasions, *marketers are trying to provide information that will help sellers quell buyer fears and give them the confidence to move forward with the purchase.*

Buying Situation 3: Preference for the Status Quo

This is when buyers are interested in buying something, but they've evaluated their options and decided there isn't any benefit in making a change or the perceived value isn't enough to move away from the status quo. On these occasions, *the primary objective is to make a credible and compelling business case that the value from buying is sufficiently greater than sticking with the status quo.*

The opportunity for marketers across each of these buying situations is clear. By developing strategies, messages, and tools that drive more leads and help build buyer confidence, marketing can have a profound impact on sales.

The challenge marketers face is the proverbial "with one hand tied behind my back" situation – trying to provide anxious buyers with exactly what they need while not knowing what they care about the most as they identify their options, weigh the alternatives, and make a buying decision – not just what to buy, but whether to buy anything at all!

What is required is deep insight into the buying decision. By understanding the mindset and behavior of buyers, marketing can anticipate and fulfill buyer needs at both the early and the later stages of their buying journey and provide sales with what they need to close more business. Understanding the buying decision enables marketers to be intentional, proactive, and impactful. Without this knowledge, marketing is often faced with "best guesses" and the changing whims of what sales needs at any given moment.

5 Rings of Buying Insight Define Your Buyer Persona

What we now need is a logical framework for our Buyer Persona that is based on the insights that marketing *really* needs to influence a market of buyers and help sellers convert more leads. As we define what an impactful Buyer Persona is, think about the five types of Buying Insight that Lagoon Oasis used to differentiate themselves in Chapter 1, plus what is required to help overcome *customer inaction* (as we've discussed in this chapter).

Buyer Personas, based on a deep understanding of the buying decision, provide the knowledge you need to develop strategies that resonate with buyers and distinguish you from other alternatives they might be considering. It's essential now to clearly define what a Buyer Persona is and what it is not.

In Parts II and III of this book, you'll learn how to design a Buyer Persona study, find people to interview, conduct probing interviews, and mine those interviews to reveal the Buying Insights that you need to make effective marketing decisions. You will need to read several chapters to learn how to achieve this result, but it is easy to explain what you'll learn through five types of Buying Insight – cleverly called the 5 Rings of Buying Insight (Figure 2.3) – and to see why this will become the most actionable part of your Buyer Persona.

Buying Insight 1: Priority Initiatives

The Priority Initiatives insight explains the most compelling reason that buyers decide to invest in a solution similar to the one your organization offers, and why others are content with the status quo. Because this insight describes in detail the personal or organizational circumstances that cause buyers to allocate their time, budget, or political capital to purchase a solution like yours, you know when buyers are receptive to hearing from you and which personas are triggering the decision to make this investment.

Marketers use this insight to define, defend, and execute strategies that resonate with buyers at the earliest stages in their decision.

Buying Insight 2: Success Factors

The Success Factors insight describes the operational or personal results that your buyers expect from purchasing a solution like yours.

1. PRIORITY INITIATIVES
Pain points that trigger a buyer to look for a solution NOW

2. SUCCESS FACTORS
Outcomes buyers need from this investment

3. PERCEIVED BARRIERS
Concerns a buyer has about making the investment, or making it with you

4. DECISION CRITERIA
Questions buyers have about your solution and capabilities

5. BUYER'S JOURNEY
Steps taken, resources trusted, and people involved in the buying decision

Figure 2.3   5 Rings of Buying Insight.

Success Factors resemble benefits, but this insight eliminates the need to guess at or reverse-engineer your messaging based on your solution's capabilities. For example, where you might be emphasizing your solution's power to cut costs, this insight might tell you that your buyer is more concerned about reducing business risks. Or you might learn that your consumer buyer is motivated by a desire to control something specific about their environment.

Through this insight, you will learn exactly what outcomes are most important to buyers and how they describe the rewards of achieving them.

Buying Insight 3: Perceived Barriers

We often refer to Perceived Barriers as the "bad news" insight, because it tells you what prevents buyers from considering your solution, as well as why some believe that your competitors have a better approach. These barriers also reveal the fears buyers have that cause indecision or concerns about moving away from the status quo (described earlier in this chapter).

When you know where the barriers are, you know what you need to do to reassure your buyer that your company or solution will help them achieve their Priority Initiatives and Success Factors.

Buying Insight 4: Decision Criteria

Through Decision Criteria, you will learn about the specific attributes of your product, service, or solution that buyers evaluate as they compare alternative approaches. Decision Criteria insights frequently surprise marketers by revealing that buyers are not satisfied with benefits-oriented marketing materials, and that companies that communicate facts are more likely to gain their buyers' trust. You may even learn that your newest or most distinctive capabilities have the least impact on their buying decision.

Buying Insight 5: Buyer's Journey

This insight reveals the behind-the-scenes story about the work your buyers do to evaluate options, eliminate contenders, and settle on their final choice. Through this insight, you will know which of several influencers is involved at each phase of the decision, what they did to arrive at their conclusions, and how much influence each of them has over the decision.

You will use the Buyer's Journey insight to align your sales and marketing activities to target the most influential buyers at each phase of the decision, through resources that help them see your approach as a perfect fit for their needs.

The 5 Rings of Buying Insight serve as guardrails for your marketing team, keeping everyone in your company on track to make profitable decisions about how to reach and persuade the buyers who have a need for solutions like the one your organization is offering. These insights from actual buyers will tell a compelling story about what your buyers want to hear and where they are seeking information as they weigh their options.

Now marketing has the credibility to lead teams to make decisions that align with their buyers' needs, goals, and concerns. Marketing also has what it needs to help sellers be more successful by understanding the outcomes buyers care about most and the fears and concerns they have moving forward.

Summary

In this chapter, we covered the following points:

- One of the biggest challenges that sellers face is *customer inaction* – a buyer's decision not to purchase anything even after expressing purchase interest.
- The top reasons for customer inaction are a buyer's *inability to make a decision* caused by the fear of messing up by making a bad decision and *preference for the status quo.*

(continued)

(continued)

- Buyer indecision is insidious – it shows up in the vast majority of sales interactions and win rates drop precipitously as the level of buyer indecision grows.
- The most successful sellers overcome a buyer's indecisiveness by establishing themselves as subject-matter experts who anticipate and address buyer concerns and calmly guide them through their buying journey rather than making them more anxious by "relitigating" the sale.
- Buyer Personas enable marketers to develop and execute strategies that build a buyers' confidence across three types of buying situations: (i) choosing the best option (no customer inaction present), (ii) inability to make a decision, and (iii) preference for the status quo.
- A Buyer Persona includes the 5 Rings of Buying Insight that reveal everything your buyers want to know as they figure out which options to consider, weigh the alternatives, and make a decision:

  - **Buying Insight 1: Priority Initiatives:** explains the most compelling reason that buyers decide to invest in a solution like the one your organization offers.
  - **Buying Insight 2: Success Factors:** the results and outcomes buyers expect from purchasing a solution like yours.
  - **Buying Insight 3: Perceived Barriers:** the fears and concerns buyers have investing in a solution, or buying it from you.
  - **Buying Insight 4: Decision Criteria:** the attributes of your product, service, or solution that buyers evaluate as they compare alternative approaches to fulfill their needs.
  - **Buying Insight 5: Buyer's Journey:** the buying steps, information sources used, and people involved in the buying decision.

3

Decide How You Will Discover Buyer Persona Insights

If, as philosopher Albert Camus wrote, "Life is the sum of all your choices," it is marketing's goal to better understand how those choices are made. Decoding and influencing decision-making lie at the core of all marketing efforts.

Yet marketing is only one of several professions that want to know how people choose one option over another. Responding to the need, countless psychologists, neurologists, sociologists, and anthropologists have written books and papers that attempt to decode the "who, what, how, and why" of decision-making in its many permutations. Market researchers deploy a variety of "qualitative" and "quantitative" methodologies to understand a buyer's mindset and behaviors as they make purchase decisions. And now, as we walk through our days with Internet-connected devices and the rapid emergence of artificial intelligence (AI), a new generation of data scientists are building complex algorithms that promise to glean meaningful insight from our digital footprints. It is dizzying to consider what all of these approaches might someday reveal or how future innovations will affect our lives.

Lacking a crystal ball and humbled by the potential for rapid change, in this chapter, we hope to simplify this topic, providing practical guidance that any marketer, regardless of budget, can employ to gain insights into their customer's buying decisions and the people who make them.

A Straightforward Approach to a Complex Question

As famed American investor Peter Lynch said, "The simpler it is, the better I like it." Based on all of the approaches we've used or witnessed over decades of trying to understand why buyers make the decisions that they do, none is more effective than one-on-one interviews with recent buyers. We don't make that statement lightly, nor do we assert it without having learned some hard lessons over the years about what it takes to *really* understand a buyer's mindset and the steps they take throughout their buying journey. This includes them revealing their most important needs, fears, concerns, and "behind-the-scenes" moments in their buying journey. It is this depth of understanding we are after because anything less will result in a missed opportunity to equip buyers with the knowledge and experience they seek in order to have confidence in their buying decision and in you.

For the purpose of developing your Buyer Persona, let's start by breaking apart and defining what we mean by *one-on-one interviews* and *recent buyers*.

One-on-One Interviews

In a one-on-one interview, two people have a conversation where one person (the interviewer) asks the other person (the interviewee) a series of questions to understand something about them or a perspective they have about a particular topic. These are open and free-flowing conversations – there are no right or wrong answers. The interviewer is simply trying to understand the interviewee's "truth" in their own words.

A useful analogy is to think about a skilled journalist interviewing someone. The best ones ask questions and continue to probe until they've revealed an insight into the person they're interviewing or a topic they're discussing. They rarely take the first answer at face value. They continue to ask follow-on questions until they fully understand the mindset of the person they're interviewing. They dig in and get their full story.

To uncover Buying Insights, one-on-one interviews work well because they give the interviewee time to talk about their entire journey – from the moment they have an initial need for a solution that you offer until the time they make a final buying decision. Unlike focus groups, where an interviewer leads a discussion with multiple individuals at the same time, one-on-one interviews give you time to ask questions, probe more when needed, and listen attentively as a buyer tells you their thoughts and behaviors at each step in their buying decision. Only this depth of discussion yields real insight.

In Part II of this book, we'll outline a unique and proven approach to conducting buyer interviews that reveals insight into their buying decisions. Based on discussions with thousands of buyers, you'll discover this approach yields interviews that are fun, informative, and indispensable in your quest to understand your prospective buyers.

Recent Buyers

The second part of the equation is who you will interview. For the purpose of your Buyer Persona, the interviewee is a recent buyer. A recent buyer is someone who has made the exact same buying decision that you're trying to influence in the recent past – ideally in the last three to six months. These are not just your current customers who have inherent biases – good and bad. These are buyers you would have wanted in your sales pipeline, but they either chose someone else or the status quo. Why is interviewing recent buyers so important? There are several reasons:

- Recent buyers aren't guessing about what they were thinking and doing throughout their buying journey. They've been through it recently and will tell you everything you need to know with confidence and accuracy. As one marketing executive and advocate of this approach recently told us, "It's like getting the answers before the test!"

- Recent buyers represent the full market you're targeting. They include the opportunities you're not seeing, or losing to a competitor, so you can be confident that the insights they reveal aren't missing important perspectives.

- Interviewing recent buyers provides the Buyer Quotes you need for your persona. These quotes give your organization a front-row seat to learn what buyers are actually saying. These quotes add depth, richness, and another level of understanding that cannot be matched any other way. And it's this depth of understanding that enables breakthrough strategies, content, and messaging.

- Interviewing recent buyers increases the authenticity of your Buyer Persona and aligns your marketing, sales, and product teams around "one version of the truth." By combining Buying Insights with actual Buyer Quotes, the legitimacy of your Buyer Persona will be self-evident to all.

  It's worth mentioning that we've participated in hundreds of Buyer Persona read-out meetings over the years and the discussions among the marketing, sales, and product teams are always engaging and unifying. Because the insights are developed from interviews with real buyers, nobody ever questions the findings. Faced with the truth about what actual buyers are thinking and doing, these teams come together to focus on actions that boost a buyer's confidence and positively influence their purchase behavior.

- Interviewing recent buyers is enjoyable for the interviewer and the buyer:

  - As the interviewer, you'll be amazed at how willing buyers are to talk about a recent buying experience that was important to them. As you continue to do interviews to complete your persona, you'll develop a sixth sense about what buyers *really* need to have confidence buying from you. The learning starts immediately, even before you aggregate findings from all the interviews to develop insights for your Buyer Persona. Enjoyment comes from facilitating an engaging conversation with someone you are trying to understand and the knowledge you'll gain to influence buyers just like them.

- Recent buyers enjoy the interviews because they get a chance to communicate something of real value to a highly interested party (you!). They don't have to guess about their thinking and the steps they took in their buying journey. They've already gone through it, so it's enjoyable and even a bit cathartic to share the ups and downs of an important decision with someone else. In fact, across the thousands of interviews we've conducted over the years, we consistently see that buyers will open up to us, revealing the trials, traumas, and triumphs of decisions that, had they gone awry, would have resulted in huge losses for their companies or personal reputations. We are amazed that the people we talk to don't want the interview to end, and that when we finally conclude, they have often thanked us profusely, as if we had done them a favor.

The interview methodology explained in detail in Part II of this book is unique. There is no other marketing research discipline that can compare with its ability to reveal insights about high-consideration buying decisions and the people who make them. Fortunately, most people can learn this simple methodology. And because it focuses on a real story, the insights revealed during the course of building Buyer Personas are not subject to any preexisting biases or beliefs.

Is This Another Kind of Qualitative Research?

In traditional market research, interviews are conducted as part of a "qualitative" study. A critical first step with these qualitative interviews is the development of a carefully drafted "discussion guide." The researcher expends a considerable amount of time and effort to build a guidebook that reduces the risk that the wording or the order of the questions in the interview might affect the responses and accordingly skew the final research conclusions.

Marketers who have previously invested in traditional qualitative research are therefore surprised to learn that Buyer Persona research is best conducted using a structure and discipline that is uniquely different. We don't follow a script, we don't prepare specific questions in advance, and we avoid introducing new ideas during the interviews.

Our objective is to listen as real buyers tell their own stories – to capture the mindset of buyers in the act of making the decision we want to influence. Fresh from the often harrowing experience of days, weeks, months, or, perhaps, even years dominated by the search for a solution to their problem, buyers can articulate exactly what triggered them to begin, and with the right prompting, reveal incredible details about what transpired as they cast a wide net for all available options before they ultimately chose one. In this construct, the researcher's role is that of a great listener, someone who is hanging on every word, encouraging the buyer to reveal exactly what they saw, heard, and did as they determined which solutions to continue to evaluate, and which to exclude.

In fact, as you will see in Part II of this book, only one question in the interview is scripted. This is the opening inquiry that takes the buyer back to the first moment in their story, to the day when they first decided to look for a solution to their problem. As we follow this real-life story, we avoid the hypothetical inquiry that diverts the conversation into the realm of guesswork and speculation rather than an account of what actually happens.

So, while it is accurate to say that this methodology is a form of qualitative research, you will want to carefully review that section to ensure that your interviews produce actionable Buying Insights.

Using Salespeople to Build Buyer Personas

Business-to-business (B2B) marketers often ask us if they can rely on their sales representatives for insights into their Buyer Personas. This is a natural question because these reps have firsthand experience with buyers and can readily tell you which influencers impact the decision. Additionally, reps who are trained to be good listeners may help you to understand your buyer's concerns, needs, and goals. Many experienced salespeople have discovered that their attention to their buyer's perceptions, success indicators, and resistance points can result in a winning account strategy. Gathering this information from your salespeople can kick-start your efforts to understand a buyer's mindset.

However, there are a number of reasons to cite caution. Salespeople are not in the habit of thinking about patterns in buyer behavior. The nature of sales engagement encourages salespeople to treat every account as unique, and any input they provide is likely to feature something about the few deals in which they are currently involved.

More importantly, salespeople witness a small slice of time in the buyer's journey, as buyers increasingly rely on their own sources to narrow their options before they are willing to meet with someone in sales. Therefore, your reps are unlikely to know anything about how the buyer navigated the earliest stages of the buying decision, a troubling limitation when this is the part of the buyer's decision that marketing needs to influence the most.

Furthermore, it's unlikely that salespeople can provide usable intelligence about the buyer's perceptions that negatively affect the outcome. The information conveyed to you from a sales representative who failed to close the deal provides a simplistic view of the situation; there are missing details that buyers won't reveal to sales reps out of fear that they will use these points to reengage with them.

While it offers a possible starting point, relying on internal intelligence eliminates the possibility that you will learn anything new. If you market a solution that buyers consider at length, there remains a wealth of additional insight available to you.

Survey Research Will Enhance Your Buyer Personas

Surveys are one of the most popular forms of market research as they provide a quantitative statistical reading of predetermined questions and choices. The results are easy to report and establish a benchmark from which to measure future results. But because they cannot discover anything that is unexpected or unknown by the survey's designers, their findings are subject to significant gaps and unintended bias. For this reason, a survey should not be used as the foundation of your Buyer Persona, but it can be used to *enhance* it in four important ways:

- First, surveys can help you validate insights gained from your initial one-on-one interviews. By surveying a larger number of buyers, you can be confident that your Buyer Persona is an accurate representation of your target market. For some organizations, this increased level of comfort is worth the extra time and resources needed to complete this additional step, particularly if your Buyer Persona is the foundation of many of your marketing and sales activities (which it should be!).

- Surveys can reveal the specific aspects of a buyer's mindset that are the most influential in their buying decision. For example, through your one-on-one interviews, you may learn that there are 15 *Decision Criteria* that buyers use to evaluate their options. This is too many to be useful for many marketing and sales activities, so the question becomes, "Which do you focus on?" Survey research is perfectly suited to answer these questions with great clarity. Doing so enables marketers to double-down on capabilities and features that are most important to buyers and de-emphasize those that are not.

- One of the first things that organizations often do after developing a Buyer Persona is refresh their market messaging or develop entirely new messaging altogether. Since a Buyer Persona identifies a buyer's most important needs, you're now in a position to develop messages that align your company's unique capabilities and features with the things that buyers care about the most. Survey research enables you to test these messages before using them in the market and fine-tune them for success.

- Finally, survey research can also help you identify worthwhile buyer "segments." For example, if you are targeting buyers who work in companies of different sizes, geographies, industries, or roles, surveying a larger number of buyers across each of these segments enables you to determine if there are any meaningful differences in their mindset or buying behaviors. If there are, you can tailor marketing and sales strategies accordingly. If there aren't, you can be confident that a one-size-fits-all approach will work just as well.

Segments can be developed from virtually any variable that describes a characteristic of a company that is important for a particular buying decision. For example, one organization we recently worked with sells technology solutions to global retailers. For one of their flagship products, they suspected that the needs, concerns, and certain aspects of the buying journey would differ depending on whether or not a retailer sold their products online versus through brick-and-mortar stores only. After developing the initial Buyer Persona through one-on-one interviews, they conducted a survey with a larger number of retailers and discovered important differences across these two segments, particularly when it comes to the outcomes they look for (*Success Factors*) and their buying concerns (*Perceived Barriers*). Based on these differences, this technology provider developed tailored thought leadership, sales enablement, and messaging that improved the number of qualified leads and conversion rates across both segments.

Because survey research is such an important topic when it comes to enhancing your Buyer Personas, we discuss it exclusively and in much more detail in Chapter 9. For now, the important thing to remember is to start by developing your Buyer Personas through one-on-one interviews with recent buyers. The insights gained from that activity alone will be a game-changer. After that, consider using survey research to further validate and enhance these learnings.

How Social Media Contributes to Buyer Personas

Is your buyer on LinkedIn, Facebook, X, or any of the other many social networks? If the answer is yes, your next question is "What is the buyer doing through that social network that helps you understand how they make the decision you want to influence?"

The nature of social media means that it is easy for you to join each of these networks and find the answer to this question. Want to know if your buyer is on X? Join X yourself and use any of a dozen tools to monitor activity for keywords related to your solution or category. Most customer service organizations are already taking this step, so they may also be able to provide this data for you.

B2B marketers can gain great insight into their Buyer's Profile through online communities such as LinkedIn. Even if you are not "connected" to these people, many will make their profiles open for anyone to read. We often visit the LinkedIn pages of the people we interview to understand their job description and education. This eliminates the need to ask people obvious questions during our interviews and allows us to devote the entire time to hearing their stories. We also find that a search for recruiting ads can help us to understand the skills and experience that are most valued by our buyer's boss.

B2B marketers will also find it valuable to monitor discussion groups on LinkedIn and other professional sites to see which topics are generating the most engagement, and to hear how people describe their concerns and opinions. While these sources are unlikely to reveal Buying Insights, you may find links to blogs, product reviews, articles, interviews, and white papers that your buyers are interested in reading. If you see a lot of engagement in any of these places, you will want to note that in your Buyer Profile.

How Does AI Fit In?

Generative AI (GenAI) refers to deep-learning algorithms that can be used to create new content such as text, videos, and other types of media, based on the data it's trained on. ChatGPT by Open AI, currently one of the most popular and well-funded GenAI chatbots, uses over 570 GB of data from a wide range of publicly available sources to train its model that produces content.

The hype train for these GenAI models and applications has never been greater, and for good cause. The idea of AI (or machine thinking) has been around since the early 1950s. However, it has only been recently that a combination of forces have come together to make GenAI models possible at scale – most notably advances in the areas of big data, computer processing, cloud computing, open-source software, and deep-learning algorithms.

Since developing insights for your persona is based on collecting, analyzing, and making inferences about relevant data you have about buyers and the buying decisions they make, it's only logical you will want to consider how GenAI can assist you. In Chapter 7, we will examine where and how to use GenAI in your Buyer Persona efforts. The possibilities are exciting but, as with most growing fields, there are pluses and minuses to consider, and things are changing quickly so we need to proceed with our eyes wide open. For now, there are two important things to keep in mind:

- First, interviews with recent buyers should be the foundation of your Buyer Persona. The day-to-day mindset and steps that buyers take throughout a high-consideration buying decision can best be captured by speaking to them. Only then can you listen and learn about all the behind-the-scenes moments pivotal in their buying journey and capture the Buyer Quotes you need to bring your persona to life. GenAI applications don't have access to this type of data as the information is rarely, if ever, made publicly available.
- Second, GenAI can help you mine data from your buyer interviews to develop the Buying Insights that you need for your Buyer Persona. GenAI can't replace the depth and nuance that human intelligence can apply to this effort, but it can increase the speed with which you identify an initial set of Buying Insights to explore further through your own analysis.

We'll expand on these topics more as we proceed through the book. But let's first focus on exactly how to develop Buying Insights through one-on-one interviews with recent buyers as this is the structural foundation of your Buyer Persona house.

Summary

In this chapter, we covered the following points:

- Develop insights for your Buyer Persona by conducting one-on-one interviews with recent buyers. Only they can reveal the behind-the-scenes story of their entire buying journey.
- A one-on-interview is a candid and free-flowing conversation where an interviewer asks a recent buyer questions, listens carefully, and probes for clarity to understand their full buying story.
- A recent buyer is someone who recently made the exact same buying decision that you're trying to influence. These may or may not include some of your own customers, but they should include buyers that chose a competitor or the status quo.
- Avoid relying on your salespeople to build your Buyer Personas. Salespeople have a limited perspective, they aren't in the habit of thinking about patterns in buying behavior, and they are prone to biases.
- Survey research, social media, and AI can enhance your Buyer Personas in different ways. These methods and tools should be considered as part of your overall Buyer Persona development plan.

PART

II | Interviewing for Buying Insights

"Go to the source. Get their story in their own words."

It's the advice that any news editor would give a fledging journalist faced with the task of discovering the facts about something or someone they've been assigned to cover.

Writers asked to compose an in-depth profile about a filmmaker, author, business leader, or politician are likely to talk to the friends, family, and associates of their subject, but they would be remiss if they didn't try to interview the central character of their article as well.

As you consider your options for conducting buyer interviews, it is helpful to think about the characteristics of a good journalist. The people who excel are innately curious, good listeners, and open to the challenges of an unscripted conversation with people they don't know.

Recall an interview by a great journalist, and you may recall that it seemed like you were listening to a private conversation. Even if the journalist was interviewing a head of state, the interviewer was comfortable with a conversational dialogue, effortlessly prompting for the next part of a story. When an answer was incomplete, the journalist took a slightly different tack with a follow-up question, persisting in uncovering the details that revealed the leader's mindset. As the story unfolded, you were privileged to gain insight into a high-stakes situation and decision that you will never personally encounter.

Many people will not want to master this type of interview. But there are thousands of successful journalists who are not Anderson Cooper, Lesley Stahl, or Chris Wallace. We hope that these next few chapters will help you to understand the methodology that leads buyers to reveal the insights you need. Some of you will feel compelled to pick up the phone and talk to buyers, others will want more training, and many will know that this is a job best left to others.

After all, how many of us can sing in tune? Practice and experience certainly make a huge difference, but many of us are unlikely to be offered a recording contract no matter how much we practice.

Timing is another dimension of the decision to do this work yourself. If results are needed immediately, an outside research firm is likely to produce completed Buyer Personas within six to eight weeks, while buyer interviewing and analysis conducted internally will likely compete with in-house marketing projects and may take longer to complete.

On the other hand, while experienced interviewers are most likely to cover all relevant aspects of the inquiry in the allotted time, marketers who know their business intimately may guide their interviews into unexpected areas of discovery.

Whether you choose to buy them or build them, you should know as much as you can about the methodology behind interviewing high-consideration buyers for Buying Insights. We hope that every marketer will use these upcoming chapters to understand how insight is discovered, analyzed, and presented for actionable Buyer Personas.

In Part II, Chapter 4 provides tips for those of you who might need to convince your company that interviews are necessary. Then we'll show you how to design and set up a Buyer Persona study with an example of an actual Buyer Persona we completed for a magnet resonance imaging (MRI) machine. In Chapter 5, we'll show you how to choose the people you want to interview and how to approach them and secure permission for the meeting. Chapter 6 details the unique methodology for conducting effective buyer interviews and recommended ways to ask probing questions to reveal deeper insight.

After reviewing these chapters, you'll be ready to set up and launch your own study with the knowledge to conduct probing buyer interviews that reveal everything you need to develop your Buyer Persona.

4 | Setting Up Your Buyer Persona Study

As much as we may like to think of ourselves as open-minded, most people's initial response to a new idea is resistance. And yet it is difficult to imagine how our lives would be affected if change was not only permitted but also encouraged.

> The abolishment of pain in surgery is a chimera. Knife and pain are two words in surgery that must forever be associated in the consciousness of the patient.
>
> —*Dr. Alfred Velpeau, French surgeon in 1839*

> This "telephone" has too many shortcomings to be seriously considered as a practical form of communication.
>
> —*Western Union internal memo, 1878*

> There is no reason for any individual to have a computer in their home.
>
> —*Kenneth Olsen, President and Founder of Digital Equipment Corp.*

Although your goal to interview your buyers doesn't register on this scale, we know that many marketers encounter skepticism or outright resistance to their plans to contact buyers and hear their stories.

It's interesting to note that the resistance you are most likely to experience will come from your internal stakeholders and that many buyers will respond positively to your request to interview them. There are exceptions of course, but despite the logical and relatively economical ideas in this book, it's not unusual to hear these reactions from stakeholders when marketers introduce the need for Buyer Personas:

- "We need to focus on [insert business or marketing priority], not 'Buyer Personas.'
- "We already know our buyers. Why should we pay for unnecessary qualitative research?"
- "We don't have time for new research, we need more leads now."

Maybe you've heard these arguments before. Although resistance can be dispiriting, it's not that difficult to construct a persuasive case for interviewing your buyers to understand their mindset. And industry trends are on your side as more and more organizations are persuaded of the great potential of Buyer Persona insight.

Persuade Stakeholders That You Need Buying Insights, Not "Buyer Personas"

If you encounter resistance to building Buyer Personas, you will want to focus on the result and not the concept itself. No one outside of marketing wants to hear about a new approach to marketing. Try to sell the idea of Buyer Personas and you may trigger a story about what happened the last time someone came in with a bright idea that was going to solve everything. Frankly, trying to sell Buyer Personas to internal audiences is a lot like promoting your products to buyers who aren't looking for them.

Now is the time to think about your internal stakeholders' persona. You may already know about a key priority that requires effective marketing, or you may need to interview stakeholders to clarify the outcomes that are most important to them. With these goals in view, suggest how a goal of particular importance can be achieved – not by emphasizing marketing research methods, but by calling attention to the way Buying Insight will help you to understand the customer expectations and concerns that your marketing needs to address.

For example, if there is a need to fill the sales pipeline with more qualified leads, talk about how you want to understand what motivates buyers to consider solutions like yours, plus the perceptions that cause buyers to maintain the status quo. If your company has a plan to introduce a new product, focus on the need to know how various buyers will respond to the new solution while helping salespeople strategize ways to overcome their objections.

Ideally, your first Buyer Persona should address an initiative that is critical and where everyone agrees success cannot readily be achieved by doing business as usual. The criticality will help you assign internal resources or the budget you need to conduct the buyer interviews. And because the outcome isn't guaranteed, your internal stakeholders will be more willing to adjust their strategies based on what you learn.

By taking on this crucial project you are diverting your stakeholders' attention away from the Buyer Persona tool and casting the spotlight on what is profoundly meaningful to them: their own Priority Initiatives, Success Factors, and Perceived Barriers.

Overcome the "We Know Our Buyers" Objection

Companies tend to start out with a fairly clear picture of their buyers. Entrepreneurs are usually prompted to start a company when a personal experience reveals a need that isn't being met. For a while, their intimate knowledge of that problem fuels the small team they build to bring the solution to market. Everyone is invigorated by that vision, and although the company remains relatively small, it is likely that each member of the team has regular contact with customers. But as successful enterprises grow, their employees begin to specialize. Gradually yet inevitably, internal dynamics begin to impact decisions. Marketers, in particular, are likely to be cut off from the customer interactions that would help them to understand their buyers and what affects their decisions.

If the founding executives are currently leading your company, they may not understand why you feel the need to interview your buyers. Or they may direct you to the sales teams who meet almost daily with buyers to understand their concerns and win those deals. In fact, there is no denying that salespeople know more than anyone else about the buyers in their individual accounts.

Should you hear that the company's internal knowledge of buyers is sufficient, it is best to avoid resistance. Instead, work toward finding common ground. If your stakeholder says, "Research is unnecessary; we already know our buyers," begin by accepting their offer to share their expertise.

"That's wonderful," you should tell the stakeholder. "This may save us a lot of work."

Follow this by setting a time for a meeting where you can learn as much as possible about the buyers. Explain that you will conduct a mock Buyer Persona interview, in which the stakeholder will role-play the part of the buyer.

Not surprisingly, any such interview will be prone to some bias, and the insights are highly unlikely to be representative of the market as a whole. But it's also possible that the stakeholder knows the organization's buyers well and can be helpful to you.

You will want to conduct the interview using the guidelines that you will learn in Chapter 6. During the mock interview, watch for any holes in the story or look for moments when the stakeholder begins to veer into a sales pitch rather than channeling an authentic buyer's voice. For example, someone who is accurately role-playing a buyer would have a balanced perspective of your solution. If your buyer-expert gives a response that sounds as if they are reading your marketing collateral, you need to call them on it. "Hold on, John," you should interject. "Are you sure you are actually staying in role here? This sounds awfully optimistic. If all the buyers think the way you've been speaking to me right now, why aren't we winning every deal?"

As the meeting continues, ask the stakeholder to next take on the role of a buyer that failed to buy your solution. This exercise will reveal the degree to which the stakeholder is aware of buyer criticism and the barriers that are hindering sales. Don't be surprised if the sales expert tells you that buyers are choosing others because your solution is too expensive. You'll want to respond by saying, "That's interesting, because we know that people choose solutions based on value, not price. Can you tell me what the buyer thinks about the fact that we can do [unique capability]? What do you think we would need to do to explain how our solution delivers enough value to justify the premium price?"

Stakeholders who encountered difficulty answering your questions objectively will now realize that there are aspects to the buyers' mindset they don't know. A better appreciation of the insight the Buyer Persona methodology can reveal should make them far more receptive.

When You Don't Have Time for Buyer Persona Interviews

It will come as no surprise that most stakeholders are focused on the immediate. Engaging in marketing research is often perceived as an unnecessary diversion of valuable time and resources. You might hear something like this: "What we really need are new leads. I certainly don't have the time to engage in a huge study. We need deliverables, and we need to get everything in gear as soon as possible."

When resistance like this is offered as an argument against engaging in Buyer Persona research, it is time to look for common ground. First, diminish any ideas about the magnitude of the project by stating emphatically that what you are proposing is not a massive study involving scores of interviews. Next, focus on the specific Buying Insights that you need before you can succeed with the goal that is an urgent priority.

As before, a mock interview in which the stakeholder plays the role of a buyer is an effective way to convey what is possible to discover through buyer interviews. When you point out that these insights can be gleaned from a relatively small number of interviews, ask them to compare this with the time and resources recently expended in other lead finding attempts. Viewed as a simple return on investment (ROI) analysis, the time and effort to conduct buyer interviews is minimal. Be sure to reinforce your goal to focus on the buyer interviews that will support this high-priority goal, reassuring your stakeholder that you do not plan to build Buyer Personas for everyone involved in every decision your solutions address.

Keep the focus on the Buying Insights you need to achieve a high-priority goal, use your insights to achieve an amazing result, and it won't be long before the tables are turned, with your stakeholders asking you if you've interviewed the buyers who are the target of an upcoming initiative. Won't that be nice?

How to Design Your Buyer Persona Study

Once your stakeholders agree that interviewing buyers is the best path forward, the next step is to design your Buyer Persona study by answering three questions that will serve as the North Star for your efforts. Thoughtfully answering each of these questions ensures two important things: first, you'll have all the information you need to target, recruit, and interview the right buyers for your study; second, you'll end up with the Buying Insights you need to better influence buyers in the target market(s) that you care about the most.

A little later in this chapter, we'll show you an example of how we answered each of these questions for a Buyer Persona study we recently completed. For now, let's review each of the questions – showing why they're important and providing you with a few tips for how to answer each.

Study Design Question #1: What Buying Decision Will Be the Focus of Your Buyer Persona?

Since you've gained buy-in to go forward with buyer interviews at this point, you should have a good sense of the product, service, or solution where you need Buying Insights the most. If you haven't yet decided that, do that first as it will be the focus of your Buyer Persona and guide all of your activities developing it.

Once that's done, you will want to write an easy-to-understand description of the product, service, or solution that enables you to identify and recruit buyers to interview for your study. There is an art and a science to this – here are a few tips that will help:

- *Use a generic description of the solution* that potential interviewees can easily understand and then tell you if they have recently been involved in a buying decision for it (or not). The only objective of the description is to screen the "right" buyers into your study and the "wrong" buyers out. A guiding principle is that the simpler and more generic the description is, the better your screening will be.

- *Don't include a lot of features and benefits in the description* because you are not trying to sell or position the solution in any particular way. You are simply trying to identify buyers that have evaluated and purchased the solution, regardless of the reason why, so that you can invite them to an interview. Understanding their mindset as they evaluated their options and made a buying decision will be revealed once you actually interview them.

- *A shorter description is generally preferred, but it's okay to use a longer one if it helps buyers understand exactly what you are referring to and eliminates any potential ambiguities.* If the name of the solution, and what it is, is typically well understood by buyers then a short, direct description will work well. If the solution is new to the market, or not something that many buyers will be familiar with, then you'll want to be a bit more descriptive to ensure they understand exactly to what you are referring.

Study Design Question #2: What Are the Key Characteristics of the Prospective Buyers You Are Targeting?

Do they work for a company of a certain size, in a certain country or industry, or have particular characteristics that make them an attractive target for your solution? These parameters will serve as guardrails, so your Buyer Persona is focused on the markets where you need Buying Insights the most. You have complete discretion to define these targeting characteristics however you wish. The important thing is to define them, so they reflect the market(s) in which you are most interested in gaining Buying Insights for your Buyer Persona. For example, if you don't do any business in Asia (or plan to), it wouldn't make much sense to interview buyers in Japan because this isn't a market you need to understand. On the other hand, if you only sell to large enterprises with 5000+ employees, then you should focus all of your buyer interviews on companies of that size.

Study Design Question #3: Which Buyers Should You Interview as Part of Your Study?

The preferred way to make this choice is to think about who among the buyers is "doing the work" to evaluate the various options and make a recommendation to the others who are involved in the decision. This person will have the most insight into the options that were evaluated and why one ultimately prevailed over all others. In the case of business-to-business (B2B) buying decisions, it's not uncommon to identify multiple functions or roles that will be worthwhile to interview, and that's okay. In fact, getting a diverse perspective on the mindset of the buying committee will ensure that nothing important is missed. We will talk more about who to interview in Chapter 5, but for now, focus on individuals and roles that are the most likely to be involved in identifying options to consider and carefully evaluating the alternatives, rather than the most senior executive involved. The latter is often the "economic buyer" who makes a final decision about whether to move ahead with the purchase but knows very little about all the buying steps that took place to arrive at a recommendation.

When answering each of the three questions, you should get as many of your internal stakeholders involved as possible to provide their input. Stakeholders in marketing, sales, and product leadership roles are particularly important because your Buyer Persona will inform their strategies the most. Their input at this early stage will get them excited about everything you're about to learn and increase the chances they'll buy into the results later on.

We never get tired of watching marketing, sales, and product people rally around one version of their "buyer's truth" when a thoughtfully designed Buyer Persona study reveals the exact Buying Insights they need to improve their strategies. Suddenly, it's not marketing's view of what buyer's want, or the sales team's perspective, or what the product team thinks. Instead, the buyer themselves takes center stage (as they should), true clarity emerges, and alignment across the organization is achieved.

Buyer Persona Case Study: Buying an MRI Machine

Since designing a Buyer Persona study is such an important first step, we're going to reference a Buyer Persona study we recently completed for a **magnetic resonance imaging (MRI) machine** buying decision and show you how we answered each of the three study design questions. We will continue to reference this study throughout the remainder of the book so you can see how a Buyer Persona is built from the initial study design phase to completion. Although the example is for an MRI machine, the same principles and types of Buying Insights can be developed for any high-consideration buying decision, including software applications, manufacturing equipment, professional services, medical devices, or any of the other myriad of products and services where buyers carefully consider multiple options to meet a need that they have.

Let's start with a little background about MRI machines so that as we reference this example at different points in the book, you'll be able to see how one step in a Buyer Persona study builds to the next.

An MRI Machine Is a High-consideration Buying Decision

Magnetic resonance imaging machines, or MRI machines as they are more commonly known, have revolutionized medicine. In the 1940s and 1950s, scientists discovered nuclear magnetic resonance (NMR) that laid the foundation for MRI. In the 1960s, researchers adapted NMR for medical applications leading to MRI prototypes and the first MRI scanner in the 1970s. In the early 1980s, the U.S. Food and Drug Administration (FDA) approved MRI for clinical use, and continued technology advancement has made it an indispensable tool for diagnosing and monitoring a wide range of medical conditions including musculoskeletal injuries, tumors, heart disease, joint disorders, and more. Because they are so commonplace now, chances are you've either had an MRI scan done yourself or know someone who has.

With the right care, an MRI machine can last 10–15 years. A new one is typically $1–$2 million with some costing as much as $3 million depending on things such as brand, model, magnet strength (e.g. 1.5 or 3 T), advanced imaging capabilities, software, installation, and maintenance costs. Manufacturers of MRI machines include GE, Philips, Siemens, Canon (formerly Toshiba), Hitachi, and others.

Buying an MRI machine is a perfect example of a high-consideration buying decision:

- They are critical to providing quality medical care, last a long time, and switching costs are high if you make the wrong decision. Prospective buyers will search for and evaluate multiple options to make the best decision they can.
- Since an MRI machine typically lasts 10–15 years, it's not a decision a prospective buyer makes frequently. Continued advancements in MRI technology mean that even a decision made a few years ago isn't the same buying decision that someone would make today. Prospective buyers will be anxious and want guidance as they learn about the different options that are available to them.
- Multiple departments and individuals are involved in an MRI buying decision. These machines directly impact radiologists, radiology department heads, imaging technicians, and the IT teams that support the technology. Add in finance, legal, compliance, and purchasing professionals that are typically involved in a large capital expenditure such as this, and there are a host of people involved in the "buying committee."

Now, imagine for a moment that you're the head of radiology at a medical institution. You realize that for a variety of reasons, your current MRI machine just isn't cutting it anymore and you need a new one.

The radiologists and imaging technicians agree. Although you've all kept up with MRI advancements to some extent over the years, your current machine was purchased a while ago and you're not intimately familiar with the full landscape of manufacturers anymore; the models and features they offer; and what their installation, training, and technical support look like.

As the head of radiology, and a prospective buyer, how are you feeling right now? You're probably excited about the prospect of buying a new MRI machine that will help the practice and your patients – and why shouldn't you be! But you're also uneasy about making the best choice possible. You have a lot of research to do, questions to ask, and internal buy-in to solicit before you can make a confident buying decision.

The scenario that we've just explained is the exact same one that MRI machine manufacturers continuously face as they try to develop strategies to influence these hopeful, but anxious buyers. A modern Buyer Persona, based on the *5 Rings of Buying Insight*, is just what the doctor ordered (no pun intended!) as it reveals exactly what prospective buyers need to know and experience to feel confident buying an MRI machine.

Designing the MRI Machine Buyer Persona Study

To design the MRI machine Buyer Persona study, let's answer the three key questions we discussed earlier in this chapter one-by-one.

Study Design Question #1: What Buying Decision Will Be the Focus of Your Buyer Persona?   The first part of answering this question is selecting the product, service, or solution category that will be the focus of the Buyer Persona. For this study, we decided to focus on Closed MRI machines that have a tunnel–shaped design – Figure 4.1. We chose a Closed model, as opposed to Open or Upright models that are also available, simply because it's the earliest and still the most common design used by medical institutions. If we needed Buying Insights for an Open or Upright machine instead, we could easily change our criteria to those models.

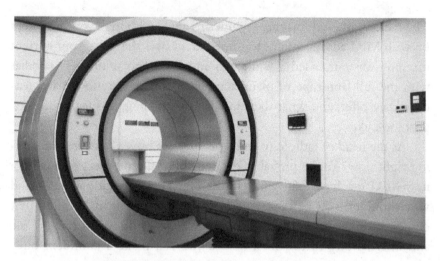

Figure 4.1   Closed MRI machine.

The second part of answering this question is describing the product, service, or solution category as simply and clearly as we can. For this study, we decided on the following: *A Closed MRI machine has a tunnel-like design and patients lie down on a movable table that slides into the tunnel.*

Because of the types of role we decided to interview (see Study Design Question #3), we knew the buyers we were targeting would know what a "Closed" MRI machine is as long as we referenced it that way. We provided a very brief description highlighting the one defining characteristic – a tunnel-like design – just to make sure.

You'll note that we didn't include anything about the varied features of MRI machines because our only objective with this description is to identify the right buyers to interview, not to sell or position the machine in any particular way.

Study Design Question #2: What Are the Key Characteristics of the Prospective Buyers You Are Targeting?   Since Closed MRI machines are used by a wide variety of medical institutions, we decided to focus the Buyer Persona on larger U.S. hospitals because they often rely on these machines to diagnose and monitor patients. Here are more details on the characteristics we ultimately decided on and the rationale for each:

- U.S. hospitals with over 100+ patient beds in their primary location or 300+ as part of a larger hospital system – the minimum number of beds an MRI manufacturer might use to identify a "larger" hospital.
- Perform 15 or more scans per day on average – ensures the hospital has an active imaging practice.
- The MRI machine costs $1 million or more – ensures the machine had robust features and capabilities and wasn't a more basic model that a smaller practice might use.
- A mix of academic/teaching, community, and military/veterans affairs (VA) hospitals – to ensure a mix across different types of hospitals.
- A mix of public, private non-profit, and private for-profit hospitals – to ensure a mix across different types of hospitals.

Why we picked this target isn't particularly important – we could have picked smaller, medical imaging practices in Europe instead if we wanted. What's important is the process of purposely defining a target market for your Buyer Persona so the Buying Insights are reflective of what you're selling, who and where you're selling it to, and where you need marketing guidance. You have complete discretion to choose the target markets that are the most meaningful for your Buyer Persona. The only caveat is that you need to be able to find recent buyers in whichever markets you choose, so avoid those where you anticipate there being no or very few buyers as it will be harder to find people to interview.

Study Design Question #3: Which Buyers Should You Interview as Part of Your Study?   For this study, we decided to speak to a mix of roles and professions typically involved in an MRI machine buying decision to get a diverse viewpoint. This included:

- Radiologists – use MRI scans to accurately diagnose and monitor patients.

- MRI/Imaging Technicians – perform the scans and work with patients.
- Radiology Department Heads – manage imaging operations, including P&L and the patient experience.
- IT Department – provide technical support for the MRI machines.

Remember that a Buyer Persona reveals insight into the buying decision across the entire buying committee, not just a profile of an individual or role. We chose to interview multiple roles in this case because in speaking with different MRI manufacturers we learned that each of these four roles would likely be involved in different aspects of the evaluation process. It's worth noting that once we completed the interviews, that hypothesis was confirmed.

Summary

In this chapter, we covered the following points:

- To overcome any internal resistance to doing "research," focus on how Buying Insights will help you understand customer expectations and concerns that marketing needs to address.
- To overcome "we know our buyer" objections, conduct mock Buyer Persona interviews with key stakeholders in which they play the buyer. If they can't answer all your questions as the buyer, or do so with difficulty, you may have what you need to persuade them.
- To overcome "we don't have the time" or "don't have the money" objections, focus on how the Buying Insights will enable you to achieve an important marketing and sales objective. Also, diminish the idea that a Buyer Persona study is a massive endeavor involving scores of interviews.

- To design your Buyer Persona study, carefully answer the following three questions:
  - What buying decision will be the focus of your Buyer Persona?
  - What are the key characteristics of the prospective buyers you are targeting?
  - Which buyers should you interview as part of your study?
- Answering these three questions ensures two things:
  - You'll have all the information you need to identify, recruit, and interview the right buyers for your study, and
  - You'll end up with the Buying Insights you need to better influence buyers in the target market(s) that you care about most.
- When answering these questions, involve all your key stakeholders, particularly in marketing, sales, and product development. Doing so will get them excited about the study and increase buy-in later.

5

Gain Permission and Schedule Buyer Interviews

With the buy-in to move forward and the three study design questions from the previous chapter answered, you're now ready to identify, recruit, and interview buyers. What they tell you will be fundamental to your Buyer Persona and serve as the foundation of the marketing, sales, and product decisions you make for the foreseeable future. Buyers love to talk about important buying decisions they are involved in. But to facilitate that, you first have to find them and get them to agree to talk to you. This may sound hard – even daunting – but don't be discouraged. In this chapter, we will lay out approaches you can use to do just that and the mindset you should have to make buyers *want* to talk to you.

Use Your Sales Database to Find Buyers to Interview

You will ideally want to create an alliance with sales as you prepare to interview your buyers. Because your interviews will focus on recent evaluators of solutions like yours, the sales organization should have a database that includes the names, phone numbers, and e-mail addresses of many of the people you will want to interview. We will soon talk about other ways to find buyers to interview, but sales is one resource that you will want to explore, especially if you plan to do your own interviews rather than outsourcing them to a third party.

We recommend that your head of marketing should initiate this request with their counterpart in sales and that you do not take your request directly to a sales representative. Remember that your initiative will be entirely new and unexpected, and that sales will naturally be protective of their relationships with customers and prospects.

We have found that it's helpful for your senior marketing executive to observe that while salespeople are trained to listen to their buyers' needs, goals, and concerns as a foundation for any presentation or proposal, marketing has traditionally worked with little or no insight into the needs of the buyers they hope to influence. Couple this with the fact that it's more difficult to persuade markets full of buyers (the marketer's job) rather than one buyer at a time (the purview of sales) and it's easy to see that marketing has a compelling reason to rectify this situation.

Now the conversation between your executives can focus on your department's desire to build more qualified leads and persuasive marketing messages, programs, and sales tools, and how those are guided by insights into your buyer's expectations. Who could argue with this logic?

Sometimes You Want to Avoid Your Internal Database

In a perfect world, your sales management would be receptive to your marketing executive's request, your sales database would provide accurate names and contact information for the buyers who influence the outcome of your deals, and you would know exactly when the decision had been finalized so that you could contact those buyers to request an interview.

But even when sales is cooperative, you may want to use other resources to find at least some of the buyers you will interview. The first reason is that these databases, in our experience, are not as clean as we would hope. We've seen lists where less than 10% of the information is accurate, creating nothing but frustration for everyone involved.

In addition, your need for buyer interviews may intersect with the activities of others within your organization. Perhaps these buyers will be the subject of interviews for a sales department win–loss analysis or a marketing success story. You won't want to have several people contacting the same person for different versions of the buyer's story, and unfortunately, the option to combine your objectives with these others isn't feasible. An interview for a win–loss analysis follows a more scripted format intended to examine and illuminate a sales organization's successes and failures. (Conventionally, either sales operations or a third-party provider oversees the interview with the buyer.) Win–loss interviews address a very different set of objectives and follow a very different pattern than the interviews you need to conduct.

Similarly, buyers interviewed for a success story tell only a selected portion of the narrative and relate it with awareness that their account will be used for a promotional press release. Their story may illuminate the reasons behind their decision, as well as details about the implementation and any associated benefits, but once again the interview does not lend itself to full disclosure of Buying Insights.

Should you become aware that the buyers you plan to contact for Buyer Persona interviews have already been subjected to a win–loss inquiry or asked for a success story, you will want to forego the request for an additional interview.

Using Professional Recruiters to Set Interview Appointments

A quick search on the Internet for "qualitative research recruiters" will turn up hundreds of agencies that specialize in finding the people you want to interview. For a fee, these recruiting companies will work with your specifications to locate buyers much like yours and set up appointments for your interviews. In addition to the agency fee, you will be asked to pay each participant an "incentive fee" that ranges from $200 to $250 for a 30-minute interview.

Should you have a budget, there are several obvious reasons why these services are an attractive option. First, you can skip the need to consult with sales and stop thinking about the quality of your database or its overlap with the needs of your other internal stakeholders. Second, you can avoid the steps we will cover later in this chapter to persuade buyers to talk to you.

However, the most valuable reason to work with a recruiting service is that you can interview buyers who have never considered your solution or chose a competitive alternative if they did. Should you want to enter a new market, launch a new product, or simply want to understand what's causing buyers to exclude your company from consideration, these recruiting resources are essential. Now, when you're presenting the Buying Insights from your Buyer Persona you can accurately claim that they are representative of the full market you are targeting, not just your own customers who have inherent biases.

To work with these companies, you will want to build a "screener" that they can use to find buyers who are qualified for your Buyer Persona study. This is accomplished by working with your internal stakeholders to define the demographics for your typical buyer, which includes all the characteristics you determined in the study design phase – things such as:

- Company size
- Industries
- Geographic location
- Job titles

In addition, you will want the recruiter to screen the participants to ensure that they have recently completed the evaluation of a solution like yours. This question should appear on the screener with these words, "Have you, within the last six months, participated in the evaluation of a [your solution category]?"

If your solution category is new or difficult to define, you can write this question a bit differently, "Have you, within the last six months, evaluated one or more of the following solutions?" and then list the names of the products that your buyer would have evaluated to solve the same problem that your product will address.

You will need to give the recruiter access to a public version of your calendar or blocks of time that you will hold open for these interviews. Then sit back, relax, and wait for the appointments to appear.

Which Buyer Should You Interview?

In virtually any high-consideration buying decision, whether business-to-business (B2B) or business-to-consumer (B2C), multiple people will be involved in the outcome, and you will need to decide which of them you will interview. The best way to make this choice is to think about which of the buyers is "doing the heavy lifting" in terms of finding options to consider, weighing the alternatives, and making a recommendation to the others. This person will have the most insight into the alternatives that were considered, how and why they were winnowed down, and why one option finally prevailed.

Marketers of high-consideration B2B solutions tend to adopt the sales organization's lingo and equate their Buyer Persona with "the decision-maker," generally the person who controls the budget. Since sales has to gain final approval from this individual to close the business, they want to focus on this person, who we'll refer to as the economic buyer.

Step into the marketing organization, however, and we can see the necessity to persuade each of the people who influence the buying decision. In a very high-consideration technology buying decision, for example, we might see an economic buyer, a technical buyer, and possibly several other buying influencers who represent the interests of the different groups of users.

Although marketers expect that they should go straight to the economic buyer – the "decision-maker" – this person is unlikely to have participated in each of the steps of the evaluation and can tell you only part of what you want to discover for the 5 Rings of Buying Insight. The economic buyer is likely to have triggered the decision to solve the problem and then handed off the nuts and bolts of the evaluation to someone else. Let's call this person the technical buyer. This person may or may not work in the technology department, but we use this label to define the person who examines all of the technicalities of the decision, interfacing with all stakeholders and managing the extended assessment that characterizes high-consideration decisions.

The more senior the buyer, the less likely that person will be able to provide important details about how the final outcome came to pass. Add to this the difficulty scheduling any extended time with senior C-suite level executives, and you can see why we don't often recommend that you interview the economic buyer.

The buyer you will generally want to interview was interfacing with your sales team (as well as your competitors' representatives) and is thus easily identified. Because this person was overseeing the entire evaluation and working with each of the stakeholders, they can give you valuable information about all of the others who played a role influencing the eventual outcome. If you want to identify this buyer for a new product, you will want to work with the recruiters described earlier, asking them to help you find the person who is most involved in weighing various options and recommending the best one.

Even if several different types of buyers are involved in the decision you want to influence, there is a point of diminishing return if you attempt to conduct interviews with all of them. There are exceptions, and if you have the resources to conduct additional interviews there is no reason not to proceed. However, the information that you gather in that single interview is the most cost-effective way to discover Buying Insights.

Interview Buyers Who Chose You as Well as Those Who Didn't

As you contemplate the universe of buyers who can relate the story about their decision, you can see that they logically fall into the following four groups:

- **Group 1:** People who considered you and chose you (your customers).
- **Group 2:** People who considered you but chose a competitor.

- **Group 3:** People who considered you but decided to keep things as they were (status quo).
- **Group 4:** People who never considered you and chose a competitor.

Before we talk about these groups, let's consider a fifth category of people: buyers who are currently considering your solution. As active sales prospects, these are people who you should not interview until the decision is complete. Although it's unlikely that anything that you might say would influence your buyer's decision, it's important that your salespeople maintain exclusive control over these interactions.

This restriction might appear to create a dilemma, especially for companies with a large installed base of customers. Inevitably, the sales organization is continuously working to sell new solutions into its established base, and marketers might conclude that this prevents them from interviewing any of those customers. This is untrue, however, and you can see why if you remember that we want to interview people about a decision that they have recently completed. Now you only need to ensure that this particular decision has been concluded before the buyer is eligible for an interview.

Now, let's examine each of the four buyer categories. For the purpose of your Buyer Persona, you'll want to consider the usefulness of the Buying Insights you can gain from each group and the ease (or difficulty) of obtaining them.

Buyer Group 1

The easiest interviews to arrange are those with buyers who selected you in Group 1 – those who have recently determined that your solution is an exact match for their needs. However, you will want to avoid too much focus on this category of buyers, as their story only reflects situations in which your organization got it right, at least for the most part. You wouldn't want to exclude these buyers from the interviews either, as these buyers can tell you which aspects of your sales and marketing interactions are most important to them. You'll want to report this positive news to ensure the ongoing investment in the highest impact activities.

Buyer Group 2

Of the buyers who are available to interview, Group 2 – those who considered you but chose another – consistently yields the most valuable data, as they can articulate how and why they arrived at the conclusion that your solution was not as valuable as someone else's. In other words, they can tell us where things went wrong.

Surprisingly, buyers who chose a competitor are not only the most useful buyers to interview, but also among the most amenable to speaking with you. Most marketers suspect that potential buyers who you lost to a competitor wouldn't want to waste time on an interview. In fact, the opposite is true – these buyers are usually the most willing to tell you what happened. They've invested a good deal of time considering your approach and would not have done so if they didn't believe that you had potential. Having determined that something about your company or solution is insufficient, these buyers often experience strong feelings, something akin to a personal relationship that ended badly, and are anxious to tell the whole, often colorful, story.

Even though buyers who didn't choose you are among the most likely to agree to an interview and provide the most valuable data, unfortunately they are also the most difficult to locate. The reason: the sales department is usually reluctant to forward information about deals they have lost.

Buyer Group 3

The third category, Group 3 – people who started and then stopped considering your solution – are fairly easy to locate. Marketing is likely to have a database that includes the names and contact information of people who attended a webinar, left contact information at a trade show, or downloaded a white paper. Alas, these people are among the least likely to interview with you. They've invested relatively little time with you during the decision-making process and are therefore relatively unlikely to spend time talking about it. The trick with this group is finding a reason for them to speak with you. We've seen marketers post signs at trade shows announcing, "$50 To Pick Your Brain" in an attempt to gather insight from buyers in this category, and they had more volunteers than they could manage. Naturally, members of Group 3 are only going to be able to tell you about the initial stages of the buying and evaluation process. If you focus too much on these buyers, you will miss many of the Buying Insights that you need.

Buyer Group 4

The final category, Group 4 – people who never considered you and chose a competitor – may be the toughest to find, but they will reveal Buying Insights difficult to obtain any other way. By interviewing these buyers, you'll learn about opportunities you would have wanted in your sales pipeline but missed out on. In addition to the 5 Rings of Buying Insight, these buyers will reveal why you (and potentially some other providers) weren't considered. These interviews also ensure your Buyer Persona reflects a full "market view" that includes opportunities you're seeing and not seeing. Because you don't have ready access to these buyers, they are best identified through a third-party research recruiting firm (discussed earlier).

Contacting Buyers to Request an Interview

With a preliminary list of contacts in hand, it's now time to start reaching out and making contact with your potential interviewees.

Ideally, you want to work with buyers who have made their buying decision within the last three to six months. Doing so will ensure that the buyer recalls vividly many aspects of the decision-making process and can impart as much detail as possible for your research. You will also want to interview people before they start to implement the solution, if that's possible. (The implementation experience can quickly overshadow the buying experience; if they are already using the product, they are more likely to want to talk about implementation aspects.) It's certainly possible to interview buyers as much as a year after the decision, but your buyer will be able to recall many more details if you conduct the inquiry shortly after the evaluation process.

The allotted time for the interview should be roughly 20–30 minutes. For a decision which the buyer allotted a few days or a week or more during the evaluation, 20 minutes is about the right amount of time. For decisions that required months or even years to conduct the full evaluation you can ask for 30 minutes, but that's the maximum amount of time to request, even though the conversation may eventually run far longer.

Sending an e-mail might seem the logical best way to approach a buyer for an interview. However, it's not recommended when making the first contact. Nearly everyone today finds managing their e-mail a chore, and inbox messages from unfamiliar names are often left unopened in a rush to attend to urgent notes from known contacts.

Instead, placing a phone call is a far more effective strategy. Chances are your first phone call will land you in a voicemail box, but its purpose is to leave a message so that the person you want to interview will be more likely to open your e-mail. By calling first and leaving the right kind of voicemail message, they are far more likely read your follow-up e-mail and consider your request.

A voicemail also allows you an opportunity to use a tone of voice that convinces your buyer that you are someone who will be interesting to talk to. Naturally, you should sound both professional and appreciative of their time. You might want to record yourself leaving this message and then play it back while attentively listening to make sure you don't sound in any way apologetic. If you feel guilty for interrupting their time and making the request, it will be conveyed in your tone of voice and give your buyer a reason to discount the importance of your inquiry. We realize that you may in fact feel guilty about asking this important person to schedule time with you, but as you gain experience with the interviews, you'll discover that buyers actually enjoy engaging in this kind of conversation, and many will want to talk at some length, keeping you on the phone far past the time you have allotted.

In your message, be completely transparent about the purpose of your call. It's a good idea to practice your opening until you can confidently explain the purpose of your call without stumbling.

When you make your call to request an interview, you'll confront one of three possibilities. You'll either connect to voicemail, get an administrative assistant, or you'll actually speak to the buyer on the phone. As most people have caller ID, you'll want to use your office phone so your company name shows up. About 95% of the time, you will be connected to voicemail; however, if you call just before the working day begins or at the conclusion of the day in the time zone of your buyer, it's just possible you may reach a buyer who's catching up on work.

Making Initial Contact via Phone

Here is a sample of what your voicemail message should say; however, it's advisable not to follow a script as reading from one often makes the message sound artificial:

> My name is _____, and I'm in the marketing organization with [your organization]. I'm calling because you recently evaluated our [specific product or service], and I'm hoping that I can get a few minutes to talk with you about your experience as you went through that evaluation.
>
> This isn't a survey; I'm looking for your candid feedback about what worked and what didn't as you went through that process. I'm hoping I can get about a 20-minute time slot in your calendar within the next week. Here's my phone number: [phone number]. I realize that it may be easier for you to respond to me via an e-mail, so I'm going to follow up right now with an e-mail, and definitely look forward to hearing back from you and hope we can talk soon.

If you connect with an administrative assistant the odds of getting the interview actually increase. You give the same introductory request; however, since you are speaking to an actual person you also have an opportunity to uncover any objections, explain the purpose of your call, and enroll the assistant's help with getting the interview. If the assistant is on your side, he or she will help you get to their boss. It's a good idea to use first names, "Tina, I would like to talk to Susan about..." And include your title if it helps. (If your title doesn't carry much weight because you are trying to reach someone in a much higher position, leave it out.) Again, the tone of your voice is important. Speak in the same tone as you would to a peer.

Following Up with E-mail

Immediately after leaving your voicemail message or talking with an administrative assistant you should follow up with an e-mail. Here is a sample:

Subject: re: _____ Interview

Hi _____,

I left a voicemail a few minutes ago but thought it might be more convenient for you to respond to an e-mail.

This absolutely isn't a sales call. I'm interviewing people who have recently evaluated our [category of solution], looking for insights into how we're supporting the market's buying process. We want to hear your candid thoughts about what worked well for you as well as areas for improvement.

Please note that no salesperson will be on the call and this isn't a survey. Your thoughts will be used to improve the buying experience for you and others in your role.

If you're willing to help me out with a 20- to 30-minute conversation, please suggest a time between Friday, October 16 and Friday, October 30. I'm in the time zone and am available starting at 7:30 a.m.

Best regards, _____

(Phone number)

Knowing When to Move On

If you get no response, you may wonder how many times you should call back and make another request for an interview. If you don't get a response, it's best to move on. If, on the other hand, you have a very short list of contact names, then you'll have to persist in trying to make contact as well as reach out to others on your short list. When making a second attempt, don't leave another voicemail. Instead, try to reach the buyer at the times when they are likely to be in their office. After you've left a voicemail and sent an e-mail, the buyer may pick up the phone, as he now knows who you are and why you're calling. If need be, call another two or three times, hoping to catch the buyer and avoid another message. But if you can't make contact after those attempts, move on to other names.

Now that you know how to find buyers to interview, we'll explore the methodology for conducting those interviews. Prepare to be amazed at how readily the phone meetings you have just scheduled will expose the surprising, factual, and useful insights that guide effective marketing decisions.

Summary

In this chapter, we covered the following points:

- Internal sales databases can help you identify buyers to interview but it's also advisable to use outside resources, such as a professional recruiting firm, to help set interview appointments.
- Use the characteristics you identify in the study design phase – such as geographic location, industry, company size, and job title – to focus your recruiting efforts.
- Interview four types of buyers so your Buyer Persona represents the full market that you're targeting:
  - People who considered you and chose you (your customers).
  - People who considered you but chose a competitor.
  - People who considered you but decided to keep things as they were (status quo).
  - People who never considered you and chose a competitor.
- Reach out to buyers by phone to request an interview, followed by an e-mail if necessary. If an e-mail address isn't available, social platforms such as LinkedIn also offer the opportunity to message someone online.
- Never feel bad about requesting time for an interview. Asking for someone's point-of-view or perspective is common practice in business today and buyers will be more likely to participate if you approach them in a courteous, professional, and confident manner.

6 | Conduct Probing Buyer Interviews

Situational clichés in magazine cartoons never seem to go out of date. There's the deserted island with the single palm tree, the new arrival greeting St. Peter at the gates of heaven, and the corporate boardroom meeting with the gigantic chart indicating rapidly declining sales.

Then there's the seeker of truth climbing a lofty mountain to obtain enlightenment from a lone acetic hermit. Underlying that situational cliché is the viewer's acceptance that all wisdom comes from asking the right person the right questions.

Perhaps not as challenging as scaling one of those cartoon mountains, learning the technique of conducting effective Buyer Persona interviews may be among the most rewarding exercises a marketing professional can master. It is, in fact, all about gaining wisdom through the art and science of asking the right person the right questions. Not only is it a productive exercise in focused inquiry – a type of critical thinking that is a valued professional skill – it is also the door to the essential insights that give marketing a competitive advantage.

With your list of contacts at hand, it's time to learn the basic principles that will allow you to engage buyers in interviews that will provide valuable information – information that buyers have never shared with your sales representatives or the competition.

Who Should Conduct the Interview?

Before we begin, let's take a moment to consider who in your organization is best suited to conduct the buyer interviews. And to make this easy, let's first talk about who should *not* conduct the interview. Answer: anyone who was ever involved in a sales call with this buyer.

If you are in marketing and are sometimes called in to assist with demonstrations, you are now disqualified from conducting an interview with those buyers. That's because we want the buyer to be completely open with the interviewer about exactly what worked and what didn't as they went through their evaluation. The buyers' attitudes toward anyone who was a part of that assessment, whether positive or negative, will influence their reflection on the decision. Additionally, buyers are reluctant to share their whole story with anyone in a sales role, knowing full well that it is the salesperson's job to use these details to open up new conversations and sell something.

Apart from this prohibition on sales doing the interviews, anyone else would be a candidate. Ideally, we are looking for someone with an innate sense of curiosity. Someone who has an intrinsic interest in learning how things work, the dynamics that determine how decisions are made, the way parts in an organization fit together, and the manner in which options are weighed. We want someone who will keep their mind open to possibilities not known or considered, and not let personal knowledge and confidence act as a blinder. We've found trained journalists are among the best interviewers. They know how to inquire about things that they haven't been immersed in. They are quick studies and can unearth the important issues by asking relevant, follow-up questions to dig deeper.

Some companies will look for interviewers who are domain experts, including people who have previously been a customer of the organization. But this approach places even more pressure on the interviewer to keep an open mind.

In one remarkable example, an engineering corporation decided that their own product specialists should not conduct buyer interviews about the decisions for their own solutions. Instead, the company asked their experts to trade places with their teammates, who were then conducting interviews outside of their own field of expertise. They had noticed that those who knew less about the product had a greater ability to respond to their buyer's answers with probing questions, pursuing the buyer's story without the taint of preconceived opinions or knowledge.

Prepare for Your Buyer Interview

You'll want to do a little preparation prior to each interview so that you don't waste time during the call asking your buyer questions that can be answered in advance. Accurately note the buyer's name, role, and company using a reliable source. (It's always nice to casually inject their name into your questions during your talk, and having it written in front of you will remind you to do so.) A scan of the buyer's LinkedIn profile will give you some idea of the person's background and current position.

You'll want some basic information about the dates when the sale or evaluation took place, as this will help you appreciate how well the buyer will be able to remember and share the details of their story. Keep in mind that since we want to discover the specifics about the buyer's decision-making process – not about the specific product or service in particular – you need not be an expert on the product, but you should spend a few minutes on the company's website so you are generally familiar with the terminology the buyer is likely to use. You may also want to consult a product expert if there are aspects about features that you believe will arise in the conversation, such as specific perceived competitive advantages.

It helps to be familiar with facts about the evaluation and its outcome: whether a sale resulted, or if the buyer chose another option. (Should this information be unavailable, it shouldn't affect your questioning. Your interview will always start at the same place no matter the outcome.)

As an aid, have a notepad handy and note in advance the pertinent information you may need to access during your conversation. It's odd how often we find ourselves unable to retrieve some facts when we are engaged in a detailed conversation and are feeling under a little stress. You'll also want to use that pad as a memory helper during the conversation.

Be sure to eliminate all distractions before doing the interviews. Turn off your cell phone, instant messaging, and e-mail alerts. Your entire focus should be on the buyer. Active listening and responding with probing follow-up questions requires a lot of concentration, so distractions are a liability.

You'll also want to have access to a good method of recording the phone conversation. Being able to accurately capture the buyer's language is essential, and making a recording frees you from taking notes and allows you to concentrate on what the buyer is saying so that you can probe more deeply into their story. Don't even imagine you may be able to write down everything the buyer says; if you try, you risk falling behind and losing rapport with your interviewee.

Finally, prior to the conversation, you should return once again to the 5 Rings of Buying Insight covered in Chapter 2 and focus on your goal. You are going to try to understand what happened in the buyer's environment that triggered their search for a solution. You are also going to attempt to learn what steps they took in order to investigate their options, discover what worked and what didn't work about that experience, and hear it expressed in the buyer's own words. We want to discern each step in the process and learn about every individual evaluation that resulted in a decision to continue to include our solution as an option or exclude it from consideration.

Get It on the Record

An audio recording of the phone call is incredibly valuable. But before you can push the "record" button, you need to obtain permission. It is unethical – as well as illegal in most jurisdictions – not to obtain consent from the person being recorded. (An audio recording of the consent agreement is all the documentation necessary.) It is not advisable to ask for this permission when you first approach the buyer for the interview. If this request is introduced during the recruiting part of the project, some buyers get anxious and may think they need to get the approval of higher-level management or consult with company lawyers.

So, plan to get the recording request out of the way at the beginning of the call. The best practice is to make this your first question prior to the actual interview, asking, "I really appreciate that you are able to take time to do this today. I'd like to capture everything you have to say, but I'm afraid that if I try to take notes I'll miss something. So, before we get started, I would like permission to record this interview. The recording will not be shared with salespeople or anyone else except the small team working on this project with me. Would that be okay?"

Ninety-five percent of the time, the buyer will say, "Sure, that's fine," and the subject never comes up again. Four percent of the time the buyer will equivocate and say something like, "Well, yeah, I guess that's okay. But I won't be able to be as candid as you would like." In such a situation you need to make a decision: should you cancel the recording or make the recording and risk the possibility that this buyer will hold back and fail to share some great details with you. We've discovered, after conducting thousands of such interviews, that the second option is the better choice. After a few minutes, the buyer will forget about the recording and the impact on the quality of the interview will be minimal.

One percent of the time you will encounter someone who insists that you can't record it. In such a case, we recommend that you continue with the interview. You won't have the verbatim quotes to share in your Buying Persona, but you never want to pass up the opportunity to listen to what a buyer has to tell you.

"Take Me Back to the Day . . ."

Once the situation about making the recording is resolved, you are ready to dive in with your opening question. This is the only question that is scripted as it is crucial for you and the buyer to focus immediately on the story of the evaluation and the decision-making process. It's tempting to try to defuse any possible nervousness with a bit of small talk that diverts the focus at the beginning of the conversation, but it's not productive. Asking, "Tim, how is your day going?" doesn't build rapport. In fact, this suggests that you aren't serious about the purpose of the call. (Sticking with our magnetic resonance imaging [MRI] example from Chapter 4, we'll be using a buyer named Tim, the Head of Radiology for a large U.S. hospital, whom we are questioning about his recent evaluation of an MRI machine.)

So immediately after you've requested the recording, dive right in and say, "Tim, I know you're really busy. Your time is valuable, so I want to get right to our first question. Take me back to the day when you first decided to evaluate a new MRI machine [or whatever category of solution your product fits into] and tell me what happened."

It's important to begin with a question about the moment when your buyer first became aware that a solution was needed – as opposed to when they first considered your product – because we are attempting to get them to focus on the moment when their organization first realized there was a problem that needed to be solved. This should have happened well before they ever encountered your product. This first question encourages the buyer to tell you about the triggering event that led to the search for a solution like yours. In our 5 Rings of Buying Insight, multiple responses to this question will lead you to understand the Priority Initiatives insight.

Don't be surprised, however, if your buyer doesn't answer your stated question and responds instead with a short list of the benefits. For instance, Tim might reply, "Well, we knew we needed to improve the quality of images we were getting of our patients, so we decided to look into a new MRI machine." Frequently, this sentence is followed by a short story about how he found and selected a solution. In three minutes or less, you could conclude that Tim had told you the whole story. But he hasn't.

Remember that the Priority Initiatives insight defines the triggering moment when the pain of living with the problem (or the positive associated with solving it) finally got this buyer's attention. We want to hear Tim talk about how this situation rose to the top of his to-do list, and what caused him to become willing to invest his time and budget on a solution like ours.

Use Your Buyer's Words to Probe for Insight

While your buyer is talking, you should be jotting notes on your notepad. Just a few keywords out of every sentence will suffice, so that you can return to some of these snippets with follow-up questions. When you do follow up, try to use the exact words that your buyer used to express their thoughts as you phrase your question.

The first probing question should be based on the benefits they mentioned at the beginning of their story. Think of this as a chance to help your buyer better understand (and answer) your question: "I want to go back to what you said about needing to improve the quality of images you were taking with your current MRI machine. I'm sure that was a goal long before you started looking for this solution. What changed or occurred to make it a priority to start looking?"

At this point your buyer is likely to give you a much more detailed story about what was happening in their organization, and they're likely to mention other individuals and roles who played a decisive role. This is where you may learn that a new Radiologist had expectations that could not be addressed, or that the Head of Radiology was constantly complaining that patients weren't comfortable in the current machine, or that the Chief Medical Officer's expansion plans required a broader set of imaging capabilities. As your buyer tells this story, you should continue to jot a few words on your notepad so that you can return later to probe into the expectations that each of these individuals communicated to them. It's likely that these senior executives disappeared from the next few scenes in the story, so this is your opportunity to ask your buyer for details about any concerns or requirements that these other individuals imposed on the decision.

Go Slowly to Capture the Whole Story

At any point in the buyer's narrative, they might jump forward chronologically in their story, skipping over the detailed insights that you need most. This often causes an inexperienced interviewer to begin probing at random moments in the narrative, which, in turn, makes gathering the entire story a lot more difficult.

Here's where your notepad is invaluable. While absorbing what the buyer is saying, jot down just a few key words – not many – about anything that captures your attention. Whenever your brain forms a thought like, "Gosh, I wish I could ask a question about this," rather than interrupt the buyer, just put an asterisk in the left column of the notepad. When you've thoroughly covered all of your questions about the earlier parts of your buyer's story, you can pick up the thread of what they already told you and ask a probing question that uses their exact words.

"You know, Tim, returning to what you just said a few minutes ago about [whatever may be a determining factor in the decision]. . ., what was important about that?"

Veteran TV talk show host Dick Cavett was particularly skilled at astutely directing the focus of the conversation back to an area that deserved greater scrutiny. He once observed, "If the person has strayed from an interesting topic, the direct approach usually works for getting them back. Just start that topic over again. Say, 'Let's go back to this,' or 'Let me steer you back to what you were more interesting about a minute ago.'"

Learning to interview is learning to listen actively, a skill that takes a lot more concentration than we might normally assume. Listening closely means not preparing the next question as the buyer is still answering your earlier inquiry. Even though the ability to multitask is a requirement stated in nearly every contemporary job description, it's not humanly possible to listen carefully, take verbatim notes about what is being said, and prepare the next question at the same time. Unskilled interviewers often move on to the next question far too rapidly, leaving follow-ups unasked, or they jump around in the chronology, asking questions about the latter parts of their assessment rather than walking the buyer slowly through every phase of their evaluation.

Ask Questions That Keep the Conversation Flowing

In addition to listening actively, enabling the buyer to talk is undoubtedly the other important interviewing skill to master. Once the buyer has given their answer and stops talking, it's important to be able to delve deeper into the story by asking a follow-on question that builds on something the buyer has said.

We metaphorically refer to this as "pulling the thread," much as you might slowly unravel a knitted sweater by tugging on a loose strand. Let's look at another point in the interview and see how that exchange might occur.

"Okay Tim, so once you and the rest of the team decided that this was the time to look for a new MRI machine, what did you do to first evaluate your options?" Let's say that he responded with, "Well, I started with an Internet search." This is not an insight, but it is an opportunity to find out how much his Internet search impacted his choice of vendors at this point in his story. Asking the simple question "How many vendors did you identify as a result of that search?" anchors Tim at this point in his story, giving you a way to define this stage in his evaluation. You can now ask the buyer about this search experience with questions such as, "What information were you hoping to find through this search?" and "Were there any websites that were particularly helpful?" One of our favorite questions is "Were any of the companies you decided to consider unknown to you prior to this search?" This inquiry helps to clarify whether this was a perfunctory search or if, in fact, the web research led your buyer to evaluate a new option.

After you've explored the Internet search experience, you'll want to find out if there were other sources of information that were consulted to find potential solutions. Most of the time, there are at least three entirely different ways that buyers identify potential solutions, and if you fail to answer this question you will miss the critical insight that reveals how buyers find solutions like the one your organization offers.

During these first probing questions a very interesting thing occurs. No one has ever before asked your buyer to talk at length about this experience, which may have involved weeks or months of painstaking research. By asking great follow-up questions in which you use many of the same words or phrases that the buyer voiced moments earlier, you're building a level of rapport that encourages them to engage with you at a deeper level. They now know that you're not just robotically following a scripted series of questions for yet another marketing survey, but that you're actually listening to them and interested in the details of their story. Your questions are as simple as, "Tell me more about . . ." or "What was important about . . .," but they have prompted them to recall details that they have never spoken about previously, and they now know that this is going to be a much more interesting conversation than they had expected.

As you walk the buyer through each part of their story, avoid thinking about the steps in the buying decision that you or your salespeople may have labeled with terms such as *research, evaluate, negotiate*, and so on. Buyers don't think this way, and these labels will interfere with your ability to uncover the whole story.

Similarly, you don't want to structure your interview around the 5 Rings of Buying Insight. This is a great format for presenting your interview findings so that they are useful to your marketing team, but it is a terrible way to get buyers to open up to you and tell you how they wrestle with the decision you want to influence. The questions in the 5 Rings don't work because they keep the focus on you and what you want to know. Your job is to keep the focus of the interview on the buyer and their story. Home in on their narrative as they explain how they identified an urgent problem, researched the potential solutions, and gradually reduced the number of options until they found the one they considered to be a perfect fit. Don't worry; if they tell you their complete story and you ask the probing questions recommended in this chapter, you'll have all of the insights you need. We'll show you how to convert Tim's story into the 5 Rings of Buying Insight in the next chapter.

Once your buyer has talked about their search to find solutions worthy of evaluation, ask them how many possible solutions they decided to include. We aren't going to use that answer in the Buyer Persona, but their answer establishes a useful transition point in their story that you will use in your subsequent questioning. As the buyer is likely to remember selective details out of chronological order, you can reference this transition moment to return them to that point in their story.

Case Study: An Example Interview with Tim

Let's look at part of an interview regarding Tim's search for an MRI machine.

Interviewer: So, once you guys decided you needed a new MRI machine, what was the first action you took to figure out which possible machines might meet these criteria?

Tim: Well, our imaging team knew who most of the major players were already and we also turned to different industry publications and white papers. So, we were already aware of maybe a small subset; maybe two or three of these guys that we thought we could check into. We had a short punch list already based on those that we were aware of, and then just did a little more research on the Internet – looking at other competitors, looking at ratings websites. No that's not the right term. Looking at industry sites that would rate the different machines and their pros and cons, checking out prices, requesting that the reps give us a call and answer questions, so a bunch of different little things.

Interviewer: Okay, so let's see . . . regarding the different manufacturers that you were already aware of, how many did you have top of mind, that you knew you want to look at? Was that a dozen, was it less than that?

Tim: It would have been like three . . . around three.

Interviewer: Okay, and when you went out on the web, and you did a search, you must have come up with a lot more. How many did you come up with through your web search that you didn't really know about before, but you thought, "These guys look interesting?"

Tim: Not as many as you'd think, because we really probably only came up with one or two more that we wanted to talk to beyond that. This is because we had a fairly specific kind of MRI machine that we were looking for.

> There were some that were too basic; in other words, they didn't really have the features or imaging speed that we needed. And then there were a few that were too advanced; they had features we didn't need, were more expensive, and involved additional staff training we wanted to avoid. So, it really came down to a pretty small set of only two or three.

Interviewer: This is interesting. Some were too basic. And some too advanced and that would mean more expense and training. On the too basic side, what would too basic look like?

Tim: Well, there were some MRI machines that didn't provide the imaging quality and speed we needed to expand our operations and improve the patient experience. Even though they might be easier to use and cost less, they didn't have all the capabilities we really needed. So those were out.

It may appear that Tim and the interviewer were just having a nice chat, but during the conversation Tim revealed a number of great insights and quotes about the resources he trusted to alert him to quality machines and his attitude as he did his web research. And at the end of this exchange, he elaborated on some of the specific expectations he had about machines that offered the right capabilities for his needs.

Your ability to uncover insight is all about watching for wording in your buyer's answers that allows you to follow up. As you practice these interviews, you'll learn how easy it is to ask the buyer to expand upon and tell you more about a comment that you jotted on your notepad. Sometimes it can be as simple as, "That's interesting, Tim, what you said about improving a patient's comfort while they are in the MRI machine. Tell me more about that . . ."

Look for Insight When Buyers Use Jargon

Another great probing opportunity arises whenever a buyer uses jargon to substitute for a more detailed descriptive explanation about some aspect of the decision or solution. You'll want to listen carefully. Some of these words are so familiar – *cutting-edge, flexible, market-leading, industry-standard, scalable, world-class*, and *easy-to-use*, for example – you may let them pass by. However, not probing on them is a huge, missed opportunity. This is your chance to uncover insight that explains precisely why this capability impresses your buyers. Undoubtedly, these same words and phrases appear in your competitors' marketing materials, but messaging that directly addresses the buyers' specific concerns cuts through the jargon and has the ability to catch their attention as if someone is speaking to them directly at the moment.

Refer to Figure 6.1 as a shortcut guide for probing whenever jargon occurs in the conversation.

Let's look at this example from our interview with Tim:

Interviewer: So, you just mentioned that you need a machine that is easy to use. Can you talk for a few minutes about what you evaluated around ease of use?

Tim: You know, just having a touchtone screen and workflows to do our imaging quickly. "Here are five simple-to-follow workflows for common imaging procedures that are easy to use instantly." That's the first thing I would look for.

Interviewer: OK.

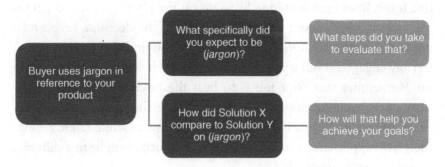

Figure 6.1 Example probes on jargon responses.

Tim: The second thing I would look for is scanning speed. I want to reduce the time it takes to do so we can get patients in and out of appointments faster. That makes it easier on them which makes it easier on us.

Another thing is coil options – you know, those things that are integrated into the table so you can adjust a patient's body positions for the scan. We were looking for advancements in coil options so we can adjust a patient's body more quickly and easily and make it more comfortable for them.

Interviewer: I didn't realize coils were so important.

Tim: One company has something called air coils. You can bend them, and they are more comfortable for a patient. If someone comes in with a broken knee, you don't have to accommodate that knee in a super tight spot. You can just wrap the knee around this coil and the patient is going to feel more comfortable. We will be able to see more patients without harming them and making them feel more comfortable.

I don't know if you can hear it while reading this exchange, but I can still hear Tim's voice as he sensed my desire to hear him out. In the course of your probing, you'll need to determine just how much time you want to spend drilling down and gathering information on one topic. If you get someone like Tim on the phone, someone who is speaking at length about a particular aspect of the decision, keep probing and let them talk. On the other hand, if you find that the buyer isn't terribly engaged about a particular aspect of their story, it is best to move on. Remember that your job is to hear the buyer's story, and if their story doesn't include any time on your website, for example, don't dally there. Buyers will impart the most valuable insight while talking about their own experience and you can get that information from a different interview with another buyer.

Make Your Questions About Your Impact Count

When the buyer mentions that they looked at a marketing resource that's important to you, such as a website, white paper, or demo, you can learn a lot by asking, "How did the information you found there impact your choice of vendors?" Because you are in a conversation with the buyer and they have already learned that you want a lot of detail, they are likely to tell you what they remember learning or experiencing as a result of the interaction. This is a far more important bit of information than just knowing that the buyer engaged with a particular type of marketing asset – this line of questioning can tell you which aspect of that asset made a decisive difference in the decision.

With high-consideration buying decisions it's likely that a key moment in the decision-making process happened when the buyer got to observe a demonstration of the product. Probing questions about the demo are an exceptionally useful way to learn about your buyer's impression of your competitors. Because this phase of the buying decision does not happen early in your buyer's story, you've likely spent enough time in conversation by this point to have built a rapport.

So be careful that you don't ruin the mood by asking for the names of the competitors or speculating about their identities. It is important to avoid questions that might provoke any discomfort, and remarkably, your buyer is likely to reveal far more detail if they haven't shared any names. Once you have those details, it's likely that you can deduce the identities based on what you're told.

You will get some of the best insights at the transition points where buyers reduced the number of solutions they were evaluating, and the demo is one of the places where that usually occurs. This point in the narrative gives you a chance to ask buyers how they decided to exclude one of the options they found in the earlier part of the story, using a question such as: "You said you started with three solutions, but you mentioned only two came in for a demo. How did you decide to eliminate that third company from consideration?"

Please carefully note the wording of this last sentence, and that the first few words are "how did you decide." This is important phrasing for a couple of reasons. First, the alternative, "why did you decide," or any question that begins with a "why" can sound a bit confrontational. And second, "how did you decide" invites the buyer to go deeper into that aspect of the story, revealing the actions they took, the information they evaluated, and the criteria that got your solution, or your competitor's eliminated from consideration. This insight is pure gold.

Probing on Who Influences the Decision

Because most high-consideration decisions involve multiple decision influencers, you will want to discover as much information as possible about the others involved as your buyers tell the story about each stage of the buying decision. As they talk about researching solutions online or consulting their peers, for example, they may talk about the other people who were involved in that research. Or they may lead you to infer that they were doing all of the work by themselves. If they haven't directly addressed that point, it's a good idea to ask a probing question. "So, you mentioned that 'we' were evaluating the input from the consultants. Who else was involved? I don't need names, just the roles of the other people."

Now you can begin to ask questions about how these other people factored into subsequent phases of the buyer's story. Through the buyer's eyes, you can identify the other roles and begin to understand their impact on the outcome. You can ask the buyer to tell you whether any members of the selection team who witnessed the demo had voiced different opinions about the demos they saw, what they learned from that demo, and how that knowledge affected their decision to continue to evaluate the two solutions under consideration.

It's fascinating that in many instances you can actually learn more about the senior decision-makers and their perceptions through your buyer's eyes than by interviewing them directly. This doesn't preclude the option to interview other buyers in the buying center, but it can give you most of the story if you don't have the opportunity to take that step.

Asking About the Perceived Value of Your Differentiators

Of the many types of probing questions in a buyer interview, there is one that requires concerted attention and care. This question has the potential to reveal significant insights, especially in instances where you know that the buyer did not choose your company's solution.

Figure 6.2 graphically illustrates a probing inquiry when the buyer has indicated that the solution that was not selected was too expensive. Your first question is "open-ended" – you are asking the buyer to recall anything that was available in the more expensive solution, but not in the one that was selected. With this question we find out whether or not the buyer can recall the characteristics that justify your premium pricing. This answer tells us whether our sales and marketing effort communicated the value but it wasn't important enough to justify the price, or if we simply failed to get the message across.

The next question, however, is even more interesting. In this follow-up question, you will want to have one or two statements that you have prepared in advance to test with buyers. You can change the statements

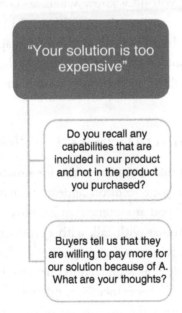

Figure 6.2 Example probes on "It was too expensive."

for different interviews – especially if you find that buyers aren't react-
ing well to the first one you try – but the wording and the manner of
framing this follow-up question is important. If it is stated slightly differently this question can sound as if it is actually a sales pitch, something
that must be avoided. Here is the question: *"We are hearing from buyers
that they are willing to pay more for our solution because it [the aspect of your
product or service that is perceived to be a competitive advantage]. What are your
thoughts on that?"*

With this question we have a rare chance to hear how the buyer
views our perceived competitive advantage. If indeed the buyer was not
aware of the perceived advantage – a not uncommon situation – make
sure not to transition into a sales pitch about your product's merits. Not
only did you promise the buyer that this would not be a sales call, but also
your objective is to understand how buyers arrive at these conclusions.

Use this opportunity to record the buyer's knowledge about the
perceived competitive advantage and whether it was viewed as important or disregarded during the evaluation. Because you are now aware
of the steps that were involved in the buying process and what resources
the buyer consulted, you now know where to concentrate your attention in the future: messaging that might need improvement; whether
sales training should be refocused; and the language buyers respond to.
And equally important, you'll be aware whether this competitive advantage is actually something your buyers value if and when they become
aware of it.

When Features Affect Decisions, Look for Insight

In Figure 6.3 we examine a similar probe for situations where a specific
feature missing from your solution appears to have been the decisive
factor. (Once again, if you are interviewing a buyer about a product that
you are not overly familiar with, talk with a product manager in advance
to learn about any capabilities that might be alluded to in the course of
this interview.) Initially, you want to find out what it is about this feature
that buyers consider of importance. Second, you want to pose an open-
ended question to gauge the magnitude of the buyer's concern about

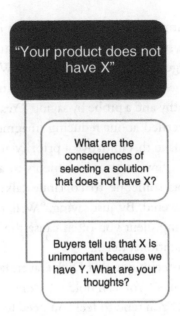

Figure 6.3   Example probes on "missing feature" responses.

this feature by asking, "What consequences might result if you selected a solution that didn't have [the missing feature]?"

In the event the product manager informed you that this feature was not included because a workaround solution already existed, you want to ask a question that is worded similarly to the one we probed with when researching price as the decisive issue. You should ask, "We have heard from buyers that [the workaround solution] is important to them because they can do [the intended outcome when using the missing feature]. What are your thoughts about that?" Again, the buyer's response will reveal a lot. You will find out if the buyer was aware of the workaround solution; whether it was evaluated; and, if so, whether it was considered a viable approach or unacceptable.

Be a Respectful Listener

Throughout the interview you always want to try to make it as easy as possible for your buyer to do the talking. Work on the flow of the conversation so that new questions logically follow up on given statements.

Adding a little empathy early in the conversation can greatly ease what follows. For instance, suppose the buyer responds to your opening question about what triggered the search by saying, "We were under a lot of pressure to reduce the time it takes to complete an MRI scan." You can follow up with empathy and a probe by saying, "Yes, it seems like medical institutions are concerned about reducing imaging time. What do you think happened to make this initiative a priority at exactly that time?"

Silence can add a few awkward moments to any conversation, but sometimes it prompts someone to continue talking when a question hasn't been fully answered. By just saying, "Well, that's interesting . . ." or by merely remaining silent you often cause the buyer to pick up the slack and give you additional detail.

This was another technique that Dick Cavett confessed yielded particularly revealing results. "You can hold someone with silence and make them go on," he said. "You tend to feel you need to fill all dead air. There are times when if you just say no more than 'uh-huh,' and pause, they'll add something out of a kind of desperation that turns out to be pretty good. Let them sweat a little and then they'll come up with something that they were perhaps not going to say."

Concentrate on the earliest stages of the buying process about which you have inadequate insight. When the buyer has covered a stage completely you can easily transition to the next stage that followed, by framing it as the next chapter in the story. Remember not to be concerned about staying on a script. By keeping brief notes on your notepad and marking reminders whenever questions arise in your mind, you can resist the temptation to interrupt and know that you'll have the buyer's exact words to use when it's time to return to that part of their story.

As the buyer skips ahead in the story, you should feel comfortable slowing down the pace by saying, "Tim, I would like to return to what you said a few minutes ago about [the topic in question]. What you said was really interesting, but I wonder if you can tell me a little more about that." Be sure to refer to your brief notes and try to use phrases and expressions that the buyer voiced earlier.

Remember, never ask questions about you, your website, your campaigns, or your solutions. Make the conversation about the buyer's experience and you'll be rewarded with more information than you could ever obtain through direct questions.

Don't make the mistake of assuming you already know the answer to a question. One of the most common errors we note when observing people learning to conduct buyer interviews is a failure to probe on the buyer's statements. When we inquire why the interviewer failed to ask a follow-up, the most common answer is, "We hear that answer all the time; I already know what they'll say." Keep in mind that you need the buyer's words and verbatim quotes so that others on your team can hear your buyer speak this thought. Even if you've heard the answer a hundred times before, hearing the buyer's response in their own words still offers the possibility of a moment of clarity that transforms your understanding of the decision-making process. As Stephen Covey once wrote, "When you really listen to someone from their point of view, and reflect back to them that understanding, it's like giving them emotional oxygen."

Once you've gathered the information during the interview it's time for the next step – using it to build effective Buyer Personas.

Summary

In this chapter, we covered the following points:

- Buyer interviews are best conducted by someone not involved in sales and who has an innate curiosity and open mind to possibilities not known or considered.
- You don't need to be a domain expert to be a good interviewer. In fact, the best interviewers know how to inquire about things they haven't been immersed in and ask follow-up questions to dig deeper.
- Learn some basic information about the buyer and their company before the interview and keep a notepad handy to jot down notes during the discussion.

(continued)

(*continued*)

- After obtaining consent from the buyer, record the discussion on Zoom, Teams, Webex, or any other platform you are using to conduct the interview.

- Start the interview with the only scripted question you will use: "[First Name], take me back to the day when you first decided to evaluate a new [Solution Category] and tell me what happened."

- Take a few notes as you go through the interview. Reference back to specific things the buyer said in earlier parts of the interview to gain further explanation and clarity.

- Go slowly to capture the whole story. Don't be afraid to back the buyer up to an earlier point in time in their buying journey if they skip over any key steps. For example, "Tim, I would like to return to what you said a few minutes ago about [the topic in question]. What you said was really interesting, can you tell me more?"

- Ask clarifying questions to gain deeper insights into the buyer's mindset and the steps they took. For example, if they indicate they went online to search for vendors, ask them "How many vendors did you identify as a result of your search?" and "What websites were the most helpful?"

- If a buyer uses jargon such as *cutting-edge, flexible, market-leading, industry-standard, scalable*, etc., ask them to explain to you what they mean by that word or phrase in the context of the solution they're evaluating.

- If a buyer mentions a resource they used that's important to you, ask them: "How did the information you found there impact your choice of vendors?" This way you can understand what aspect of that resource made a real difference in the decision.

- Be a respectful listener and show empathy. The buyer will be more open and forthright as a result.

PART III

Creating Your Buyer Persona

If you've been conducting interviews yourself, listening to the recordings, or reading the transcripts you're undoubtedly starting to get a real sense of what your prospective buyers need to know and experience to feel confident buying from you. They've talked about the challenges and circumstances that made them look for a solution just like yours and the outcomes they expect. They've revealed their buying fears, concerns, and requirements. And they've disclosed all the steps, resources, and people involved in their buying decision. You've taken the first step to walk in their shoes and understand just what they need to feel assured in their buying decision.

Now is the time to dig into your interview transcripts, pull out the insights you need for your Buyer Persona, and organize them in a way that makes it easy for everyone to understand and use whether it be marketing, sales, product management, or any other function that needs to meet the needs of prospective buyers.

In Chapter 7, we'll show you how your intelligence should be processed, organized, and analyzed in a format that helps you classify the most important information and discern where each pertinent gem of knowledge belongs in the persona's Buying Insights. In Chapter 8, we'll provide examples of how to communicate and present your Buyer Persona insights for impact and identify top themes that will resonate with buyers. Chapter 9 – a new chapter in this revised and expanded edition – provides guidance for how to conduct survey research to enhance your Buyer Persona, including determining which buyer expectations are the most (and least) important, testing value proposition and messaging concepts, and identifying buyer segments within your persona. Although survey research isn't required to get immense value from your Buyer Persona insights, it can enhance the impact that they have.

7

Mine Your Interviews for Buying Insights

It's a familiar scene from countless investigative police TV shows. The chief detective assembles the team and presents the evidence on a bulletin board. There are forensic photographs and images of witnesses and suspects. Pinned next to them is a detailed map of the crime scene, a timeline, photocopies of key evidence, and selected witness statements. This visual image is a powerful dramatic device that helps all observers understand the relevant personalities and clues (as well as red herrings) in the story.

Following your buyer interviews, you are going to engage in an exercise that has some parallels with the work of the chief detective. The stories we capture during our interviews will synthesize and prioritize the key elements of a narrative that has been a mystery until now.

But while the chief detective subjects the suspects' stories to a systematic analysis that gradually eliminates everyone except the prime suspect, we will do almost the reverse. We will combine all of the stories to create a single narrative that represents the mindset of a group of buyers that think alike. When we are done, we will have a factual description of our person (or persons) of interest, and a story that details their expectations, decision-making process, and thinking as they approach the decision you want to influence.

You Need Fewer Interviews Than You Think

As you interview your first few buyers, it's likely you will begin to hear very similar stories. You may get virtually identical answers to your questions about the buyers' Priority Initiatives, or people may have very similar concerns and barriers to choosing your solution.

However, before you begin to compile and aggregate your findings, it's a good rule to complete at least ten buyer interviews. This doesn't mean that you won't complete additional interviews, but this is a good time to be aware of patterns and to compile your existing results.

While you are building your confidence in the interviewing methodology that we discussed in the last chapter, initiating this step after just a few interviews will help you to identify areas of the buyer's stories where you haven't probed deeply enough. Don't worry about returning to the people you have already interviewed. Just make sure to focus on the missing areas in your upcoming interviews.

Once you are proficient with the interview techniques, you may be surprised to learn how few interviews it takes to discover all 5 Rings of Buying Insight from Chapter 2. Your decision about how many interviews to conduct will be easier if you think about Buyer Persona insight as a tool to cut through the clutter and tell you exactly what you need to do. Now you can see that marketing based on intuition and guesswork is a blunt ax, and that insights culled from a small group of interviews is akin to a Swiss Army knife. This degree of acuity is relatively easy to achieve and much sharper than anything you've ever had in your toolkit. For most marketing decisions and objectives, this is perfectly aligned with the job at hand.

Should you be a marketer working in-house, we recommend that you continue to conduct buyer interviews on a regular basis, attempting to complete one each month. You are unlikely to gain significant new insights from these interviews in the near term, but when change does occur you will be the first to know. In addition, you will have the credibility at internal meetings to say, "I just spoke to a buyer last week, and she said . . ."

Steps for Developing Buying Insights from Your Interviews

Like the chief detective, we need to categorize and prioritize our research into a succinct, easily understood format so that we can be sure we didn't miss anything. We have limited resources available to locate and capture our suspects, so we must convert reams of interview data into a succinct and revealing story that motivates the team, aligning everyone to execute the most productive strategy.

Step 1: Mark Up Your Interview Transcripts

As soon as you complete an interview, send your recorded discussion to a transcription service to have it converted into a written document. If you're using an online platform to conduct the interview – such as Zoom, Teams, Webex, and others – you can also use the real-time transcription feature that these platforms typically have.

Don't skip this step, as your interview transcripts contain the verbatim quotations that will make your Buyer Personas speak from the heart, voicing the real concerns and attitudes that your stakeholders need to hear.

With the first transcript open on your computer, read the interview from the beginning. When you find a quotation that answers one of the questions in the 5 Rings of Buying Insight, use the "comments" feature in your word processing software to highlight the quotation and label it with the relevant insight – Figure 7.1.

Because you started the interview by asking buyers about their Priority Initiatives, you are likely to find quotations early on that help you to convey the triggering events and the people that set the decision-making process in motion. Mark any quotations that answer this question with a "PI" for Priority Initiatives.

Jared: So, essentially the MRI machine was at the end of life. So, at that point, there was need for an upgrade. So, there was a decision to start looking into new equipment. There were maintenance issues, and issues with downtime, quality of images, throughput, and compatibility with the network. **Priority Initiatives (PI).**

Interviewer: What else were you hoping to achieve with this new machine? How would it benefit your organization?

Jared: Probably increased throughput, increased number of patients scheduled, and then also increased or improved diagnosis of disease processes. **Success Factors (SF).**

Interviewer: Anything else that was sort of on your wish list with this new machine that we haven't already touched on? Anything else you were hoping to achieve that would spell success?

Jared: Multiple compatibility. So, depending on the machine you have, you need to get multiple different sets of coils, whether it be for extremity versus brain versus spine versus abdomen. So, compatibility with multiple different options and sequences would be helpful. **Success Factors (SF).**

Interviewer: You talked about specific offerings and specific features. Let's talk about what you learned about these providers that really helped you start to narrow things down.

Jared: I looked at their sequences available, their compatibility in terms of coils that were available on the market, cost of coils, bundling of the different equipment, looking at the different sequences that were available on the market for manufacturer. **Decision Criteria (DC).**

Interviewer: What else? You mentioned scanning time earlier.

Jared: Yes, you also look at the time for the sequences, how long it takes for each individual one. Say, for example, you might do a sequence for a brain MRI. Say Provider X might take 12 minutes versus Provider Y at 14 minutes. And those small nuances and their algorithms for their sequences might change the image quality, just a hair. And then it also changes the timing and allows for different amounts of procedures to be done. [It] All plays a large role in overall workflow. **Decision Criteria (DC).**

Figure 7.1   Example interview transcript markup.

As you continue to read your buyer's story, you will find quotations about the changes buyers expected to gain from this solution – these should be marked "SF" for Success Factors. Remember that Success Factors sound like benefits statements, so keep an eye out for specific business or practical outcomes, as well as personal aspirational statements.

You will find Perceived Barriers "PB" insights throughout the interview, and especially in the places where you probed about how the buyer eliminated a few solutions from consideration. Buyers will also speak early in their story about the barriers that prevented them from addressing this problem much sooner. Perceived Barriers often focus on people who got in the way, previous negative experiences, or capabilities that are missing from some solutions.

The questions that probed on how buyers eliminated options or why they kept certain solutions under consideration will also give you quotations that you can mark as Decision Criteria "DC." These differ from the other insights because they describe the specific features or capabilities of the company or solution that were most important to your buyer. You will also find these quotations in response to your probing questions about what the buyer wanted to learn while reading a white paper, visiting a website, or attending a demo.

As you read through your buyer's story, mark quotations "BJ" for the Buyer's Journey insight whenever they describe who was involved in the decision and what the buyer did to evaluate their options.

Not all the insights you mark on the transcript will fall easily within these five neat categories; some comments may encompass two insight categories simultaneously. In particular, the differences between Success Factors and Decision Criteria seem to cause confusion.

As a shorthand aid, think of Success Factors as benefits: scenarios that buyers believe will change after they complete this purchase. These might range from results that directly relate to the company's Priority Initiatives – for instance, growing revenue by enabling a more personalized experience for online customer transactions – to things that might impact the buyer's career or the company's reputation. Remember that Success Factors communicate your buyers' specific expectations for the *outcomes* that matter most to them.

By contrast, Decision Criteria are the *capabilities* that your buyers evaluate regarding each of the solutions they are considering. These insights tell you what tips the balance in favor of a particular option during the decision-making process. In the case of hardware or software, these are often specific features or functions that matter decisively to the buyer. Buyers might also emphasize the importance of a service function, for instance, "We want to work with people who treat us like we're important." Decision Criteria are the attributes of the solution that buyers believe they need in order to achieve their Success Factor outcomes.

Another way of separating these two insight categories is to think of Decision Criteria as answering the *what* and *how* (as in "What aspect of the solution is critically decisive, and how does it do this?"), while Success Factors answer the *why* ("Why is this aspect important to the organization?").

There are situations in which a buyer's Success Factors and Decision Criteria are linked. Let's look at our magnetic resonance imaging (MRI) machine example. One buyer we interviewed about his search told us:

> We looked at the time for the sequences – how long it takes for each individual one. For example, for a brain MRI, Company D takes 12 minutes versus Company B who takes 14 minutes. Those small nuances and their algorithms are important. They change the timing, and it allows for different numbers of procedures to be done in a day, which plays a large role in our overall workflow and revenue.

We could capture the first three sentences in this quotation as one of the Decision Criteria because they answer the *what* question (scanning times). But the last sentence would be captured under Success Factors because it answers *why* this feature is important (enables more procedures and revenue).

As you scrutinize more buyer interviews and contemplate how the insights revealed during the course of the conversations define the buyer's mindset, you will become better attuned to distinguishing the important yet subtle differences between these two crucial insight categories.

Step 2: Organize the Story Based on Buying Insights

You now need to choose which of the many quotations that you have highlighted will best communicate the insights you captured during the interviews. You will likely have dozens of quotations highlighted in each interview, but you can't expect your stakeholders to read all of them. Instead, you need to choose the most insightful quotations, those where the buyer disclosed the details and emotions that had the greatest impact on their choice of solutions.

The easiest way to do this is to use a spreadsheet program, such as Microsoft® Excel®, to build an "Insights Aggregator" that is made up of five tabulated worksheets, naming one for each of the 5 Rings of Buying Insight – see Figure 7.2.

On each worksheet, label Column A for Buyer Quotes. The second, Column B, is where you will note the interview that was the Source of the quotation. Column C is used to create a shorthand summary of the Main Points contained in the insight quotation. Column D is where you will write your final "Buying Insight Headline" that you'll use in your Buyer Persona.

For the first part of this process, we'll fill in only Columns A and B. After we have all of the quotations from all of the interviews pasted into these two columns, we'll return to Columns C and D where we will begin to analyze the quotations we've collected and prepare our Buying Insights.

Once you have the worksheet built, start with your first marked-up interview and begin to paste quotations into Column A of the Insights

	A	B	C	D
1	**Decision Criteria:** Identify the top three to five factors that this Buyer Persona uses to compare alternative approaches/options and make a decision. If this Buyer Persona is involved throughout the Buyer's Journey, these criteria may change at different stages of the process.			
2	**Buyer Quotes**	**Source**	**Main Point**	**Buying Insight Headline**
3				

Priority Initiatives   Success Factors   Perceived Barriers   Decision Criteria   Buyer's Journey

Figure 7.2 Insights Aggregator spreadsheet.

Aggregator. As you insert the quotation into the worksheet, don't forget to identify the source of the interview (in Column B) where this quotation originated, as you will need that detail in the steps that follow.

You should be able to move quickly through each interview, copying quotations in whatever order they appear in the interview and pasting quotations into the correct tab of your worksheet. As you move through this step, you may notice that you marked up quotations that are not as useful as those you marked in other parts of the interview. Feel free to skip any quotations that are not compelling, or if you prefer, paste them all into the worksheet and attend to the culling of less useful quotations once they are all in one place.

You'll note that our illustration of the tabbed worksheet includes a summary definition of each of the 5 Rings of Buying Insight at the top of each page. As you cut and paste your buyer's quotations into this worksheet, these will help you remember the questions your buyer's quotations are meant to answer. When you complete this step, your worksheet will look like the one in Figure 7.3, that shows an example from our MRI machine buyer interviews.

Step 3: Summarize the Main Point of Each Quotation

Once you have pasted the quotations into the relevant parts of the Insights Aggregator, it is time to write a short statement for each of the quotations. Starting with the Priority Initiatives tab, read each quotation and write a few words in Column C, the "Main Point" column of the Insights Aggregator – that communicates the key point explaining what triggered the buyer's search for a solution. As you continue to read the quotations you have selected, you should adjust the wording of your Main Points so that similar quotations can be listed together. Once you have completed this step on your Priority Initiatives worksheet, you can use the sort feature in your spreadsheet program to group related quotations together. Repeat this for each of the other four insights and your worksheet will look like Figure 7.4.

A	B	C	D
	Source	Main Point	Buying Insight Headline

Decision Criteria: Identify the top three to five factors that this Buyer Persona uses to compare alternative approaches/options and make a decision. If this Buyer Persona is involved throughout the Buyer's Journey, these criteria may change at different stages of the process.

Buyer Quotes

Our radiologist has looked at a lot of images that have been submitted for accreditation and his input on image quality is well respected, so we took that into account. Based on his practice and protocols, he felt that the sequences and image quality of Company B was better than Company C. — Bill, MRI Dept. Head

Company B's spine coil is integrated into the table, just like Company C. The head and neck coil made great strides since the last model, we are able to adjust the head so if a patient has a humpback or if they are uncomfortable in the scanner, you can adjust the coil. This makes patients more comfortable in the scanner. They put a lot of effort into comfort, which is a win. — Albert, Radiologist

Overall, when Company C installs a system, I feel like the quality of the workmanship is superior. When a magnet gets installed by Company C, you have to make sure the room is sealed properly and the magnet is level with the floor. It's a week's worth of installation making sure that everything is up and running properly. I've never had a problem with Company C, other than a drastic issue like a power failure or something unavoidable. There tends to be more service calls with the installation of a Company A machine than with Company C, in my experience. — Vince, MRI Tech.

Figure 7.3 Insights Aggregator – cut and paste quotations.

A	B	C	D
Radiologists and radiology techs tend to have a preference for Company A based on their after sales support. They are just more responsive and more collaborative. They understand our needs and our challenges. They know if a machine goes down, they can fix it quickly. That's important to us.	Emily, IT		
We have one of the louder scanning bores, whereas now the industry standard is silent scanning. It has ambient noise rather than the high volumes that our current scanner ran on. The technology has changed, so we wanted that ambient noise feature.	Ed, MRI Dept. Head		
Is this the top of the line scanner or does this have the latest and greatest technology to build on in the future? Company B's platform hasn't changed much. If we had chose Company B, we would have been just fine, but I felt like the Company C scanner took the technology to another level. We won't have to compete with industry standards, we will be leading it. In three years, the Company B machine will be obsolete, but the Company A will be leading the game at that point.	Diane, MRI Dept. Head		

Figure 7.3 (*Continued*)

A	B	C	D
			Buying Insight Headline
	Source	Main Point	
Decision Criteria: Identify the top three to five factors that this Buyer Persona uses to compare alternative approaches/options and make a decision. If this Buyer Persona is involved throughout the Buyer's Journey, these criteria may change at different stages of the process.			
Buyer Quotes			
Our radiologist has looked at a lot of images that have been submitted for accreditation and his input on image quality is well respected, so we took that into account. Based on his practice and protocols, he felt that the sequences and image quality of Company B was better than Company C.	Bill, MRI Dept. Head	Image Quality	
We pay close attention to the sharpness of images. I'm concerned about the MRIs of the brain, spine, and joints, because that's my focus. Company D looks better than Company A, the image is sharper and contrast is a little better. There are also certain differences in sensitivities in terms of sequences. We wanted to have a machine that showed us images like gradient echo sequences which allows us to look for blood in the brain. Company D has their proprietary sequence that is more sensitive to detection of prior micro hemorrhages from concussions.	Albert, Radiologist	Image Quality	
I've had challenges with Company D, you don't have as much freedom to reconstruct the 3D imaging from one plane to another. It just didn't have the higher-functioning imaging platform that they wanted or needed. Company B allows for higher-functioning imaging when you're trying to push the gradients to the limit, the quality is better. From a physicist perspective, I've heard that the imaging on a Company B machine is superior.	Vince, MRI Tech.	Image Quality	

Figure 7.4   Insights Aggregator – write main points.

A	B	C	D
Radiologists and radiology techs tend to have a preference for Company A based on their after sales support. They are just more responsive and more collaborative. They understand our needs and our challenges. They know if a machine goes down, they can fix it quickly. That's important to us.	Emily, IT	Tech Support	
Company B was one that we kept on our list, because we've had some significant service issues with Company D. That has left a sour taste in people's mouths. Company D was having a hard time with their service and support, they had poor response times and that soured us from getting one of their magnets. Company B service is great and I know they support our neighboring hospitals, so that played a part in our decision.	Ed, MRI Dept. Head	Tech Support	

Figure 7.4 *(Continued)*

Next, use your best copywriting skills to help you create your final "Buying Insight Headlines." Many stakeholders will scan these headlines without reading the buyer's quotations, so you will want to include as much detail as possible. We've found it useful to follow the organizing format of the spreadsheet with separate pages devoted to each of the 5 Rings of Buying Insight, and to write each headline as if the buyer was directly answering that Ring's question.

For example, you have a group of related quotations that define Decision Criteria: the key questions that buyers use to evaluate and compare their options. On your spreadsheet you summarize the Main Point as "Image Quality." However, to prepare these insights for your Buyer Persona, you should write these as a "Buying Insight Headline" in the voice of a person who is directly asking the Decision Criteria question. For this group of quotations, you might write a headline such as, "How sharp, clear, and detailed is the imaging quality?" The goal is to create a headline in Column D that conveys the core idea with conviction and urgency. Repeat this for each of the other four insights and your worksheet will look like Figure 7.5.

Step 4: Select Buyer Quotes for Each Buying Insight

Now it's time to select the Buyer Quotes and Buying Insight Headlines that you will use in your Buyer Persona. Once your worksheet is sorted by the Buying Insight Headline, a quick scan will tell you how many quotations you have for each of the headlines you created in Column D.

First, have a look at headlines where you have several quotations, checking to see if they each came from different buyer interviews, as will be indicated in Column B. If two or more of the quotations are from the same buyer interview, delete the one that is least useful and retain the one that conveys the most compelling detail about that buyer's expectations. You don't want to use multiple quotations from one buyer interview to support any Buying Insight.

A	B	C	D
Decision Criteria: Identify the top three to five factors that this Buyer Persona uses to compare alternative approaches/options and make a decision. If this Buyer Persona is involved throughout the Buyer's Journey, these criteria may change at different stages of the process.			**Buying Insight Headline**
Buyer Quotes	**Source**	**Main Point**	
Our radiologist has looked at a lot of images that have been submitted for accreditation and his input on image quality is well respected, so we took that into account. Based on his practice and protocols, he felt that the sequences and image quality of Company B was better than Company C.	Bill, MRI Dept. Head	Image Quality	How sharp, clear, and detailed is the imaging quality?
We pay close attention to the sharpness of images. I'm concerned about the MRIs of the brain, spine, and joints, because that's my focus. Company D looks better than Company A, the image is sharper and contrast is a little better. There are also certain differences in sensitivities in terms of sequences. We wanted to have a machine that showed us images like gradient echo sequences which allows us to look for blood in the brain. Company D has their proprietary sequence that is more sensitive to detection of prior micro hemorrhages from concussions.	Albert, Radiologist	Image Quality	How sharp, clear, and detailed is the imaging quality?
I've had challenges with Company D, you don't have as much freedom to reconstruct the 3D imaging from one plane to another. It just didn't have the higher-functioning imaging platform that they wanted or needed. Company B allows for higher-functioning imaging when you're trying to push the gradients to the limit, the quality is better. From a physicist perspective, I've heard that the imaging on a Company B machine is superior.	Vince, MRI Tech.	Image Quality	How sharp, clear, and detailed is the imaging quality?

Figure 7.5 Insights Aggregator – write key insight headlines.

A	B	C	D
Radiologists and radiology techs tend to have a preference for Company A based on their after sales support. They are just more responsive and more collaborative. They understand our needs and our challenges. They know if a machine goes down, they can fix it quickly. That's important to us.	Emily, IT	Tech Support	How responsive and effective is your after-sale technical support?
Company B was one that we kept on our list, because we've had some significant service issues with Company D. That has left a sour taste in people's mouths. Company D was having a hard time with their service and support, they had poor response times and that soured us from getting one of their magnets. Company B service is great and I know they support our neighboring hospitals, so that played a part in our decision.	Ed, MRI Dept. Head	Tech Support	How responsive and effective is your after-sale technical support?

Figure 7.5 *(Continued)*

Next look to see if you still have any Buying Insight that have four or more quotations from different buyers. If these are all compelling quotations, think about whether you could write even more detailed, compelling headlines by assigning two of the quotations to a newly written Buying Insight. If you're able to do this, the insights may be even more specific and valuable to your marketing team in terms of defining buyer expectations.

Conversely, for Buying Insights that have only one quotation, consider consolidating these under a Buying Insight that expresses what two or more of these quotations have in common. But don't force a connection if one doesn't exist. For quotations that are truly outliers, leave them on the spreadsheet until additional data supports their inclusion in your Buyer Persona.

When you have completed the interviews and organized your findings based on the 5 Rings of Buying Insight, you have a very clear picture of the factors that drive your buyer's decisions. You have probably mined more than 100 pages of transcribed interviews to find the quotations that best depict your buyers' mindsets as they wrestled with the decisions you want to influence. Through these quotations, you will be able to reveal the essence of your buyer's stories in a relatively brief narrative that will guide your team's most critical marketing decisions.

Using AI to Mine Your Interviews for Insights

If you only develop Buyer Personas occasionally, we recommend using the approach outlined in this chapter to mine interviews for insights and develop your buyer's narrative. Because there is some nuance to the analysis that is best teased out through human intelligence, this ensures nothing is missed, your headlines are as accurate and compelling as they can be, and you've identified the best quotes to tell your buyer's stories. The relatively modest investment in time is worth the extra value you'll get from this deeper and more thoughtful analysis.

However, if you develop Buyer Personas more than occasionally, you may wish to explore Generative AI (GenAI) platforms, such as

ChatGPT and others, where you can "feed" transcripts into a model to get a preliminary idea of Buying Insight themes that are emerging. GenAI can't replace the depth and nuance that human intelligence can apply to this effort, but it can increase the speed in which you identify an initial set of Buying Insights to explore further through your own analysis.

There are no defined rules for how to leverage these GenAI platforms to analyze transcripts, and best practices will continue to evolve, but we have found the following steps do a good job of revealing a preliminary set of Buying Insights across each of the 5 Rings:

Upload or copy and paste your transcripts into the GenAI platform and provide it with the following instructions:

1. Instruct the model: "Utilize only the provided transcripts to answer the following questions." This ensures the model only uses data from the transcripts in its analysis.
2. Using the MRI machine buyer interviews as an example, use the following prompts for each of the 5 Rings of Buying Insight:
   - **Priority Initiatives:** "What are the immediate needs that triggered the decision to purchase a new MRI machine now?"
   - **Success Factors:** "What outcomes did buyers need to achieve with the new closed MRI machine? Include mentions of performance, operations, costs, etc."
   - **Perceived Barriers:** "What concerns did buyers have about making the investment or caused them to choose a different provider?"
   - **Decision Criteria:** "What questions did buyers have about the closed MRI machine and its capabilities? What questions did they have regarding the companies themselves?"
   - **Buyer's Journey:** "Who was involved in the evaluation and what trusted resources were used to gain information about the MRI machine? Include mentioned resources, such as vendor websites, physical site visits, conferences, etc., with context of why those resources were trusted and what was learned while utilizing those resources."

3. Instruct the model: "Annotate the source of the output." This sources the buyer transcript(s) used to produce the output so you can cross-reference them for accuracy and additional context.

Putting it all together, here is an example of a full prompt you might use to reveal an initial set of Priority Initiatives insights:

Utilize only the provided transcripts to answer the following question: What are the immediate needs that triggered the decision to purchase a new MRI machine now? Annotate the source of the output.

Since GenAI will continue to evolve, and prompt engineering is a growing field whereby data analysis is used to improve prompts within different platforms, the aforementioned guidance should be used as a starting point. You should feel confident that if the interviews you completed provide detailed and accurate information about the mindsets and behaviors of buyers, there are GenAI prompts that will yield the preliminary Buying Insights you need. Keep experimenting and document where you have success so you can leverage these best practices in future studies.

If you do decide to leverage GenAI in your efforts, use caution feeding transcripts into platforms that aren't proprietary or where your technical team hasn't set up a secure version of it for you to use internally. You've made an investment in time and resources to develop your Buyer Persona and you wouldn't want your interview data inadvertently shared outside of your organization.

Summary

In this chapter, we covered the following points:

- After you complete a buyer interview, have it transcribed into a written document that you can use to mine the discussion for Buying Insights.

- Use a four-step approach to mine the transcripts for Buying Insights:
  - **Step 1: Mark Up Your Interview Transcripts:** Identify and categorize Buyer Quotes across each of the 5 Rings of Buying Insight.
  - **Step 2: Organize the Story Based on Buying Insights:** Using an Insights Aggregator tool that you can create in any spreadsheet program – copy and paste each quote, note the interview it came from, and create a shorthand summary of main points contained in the quotation.
  - **Step 3: Summarize the Main Point of Each Quotation:** Use your best copywriting skills to write your final "Buying Insight Headline." Many stakeholders will scan these headlines without reading the Buyer's Quotes, so you will want to include as much detail as possible.
  - **Step 4: Select Buyer Quotes for Each Buying Insight:** For each Buying Insight, identify the best Buyer Quotes that support it; choose only one quote per buyer by retaining the one that conveys the most compelling detail about that particular buyer's expectations.

- Use this four-step approach if you only develop Buyer Personas occasionally. If you do more frequent studies, consider using GenAI as a first step for identifying an *initial* set of Buying Insights followed by further exploration through your own (human) analysis.

8 | Communicate Buying Insights for Impact

Once you have completed the Insights Aggregator, your next step is to communicate the Buying Insights on your spreadsheet in a format that helps your company align its strategies with what you've learned.

Marketers enjoy a lot of creative options for these presentations. In addition to PowerPoint, we've seen posters, infographics, and elaborate intranet sites where internal teams can find the Buyer Personas that will help them make decisions. Any or all of these are appropriate, bearing in mind that you want to choose a format that is most helpful to your internal audience, even if it does not earn you any design awards.

Presenting the 5 Rings of Buying Insight to Others

The most common way to present Buyer Personas is through presentation software such as PowerPoint (.PPT), Google Slides, Prezi, or others. Figures 8.1–8.7 are examples of the PPT template that we use to summarize insights for each of the 5 Rings of Buying Insight, completed

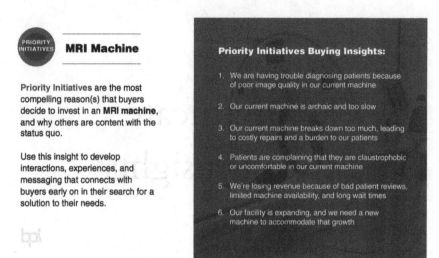

Figure 8.1   MRI machine Priority Initiatives summary.

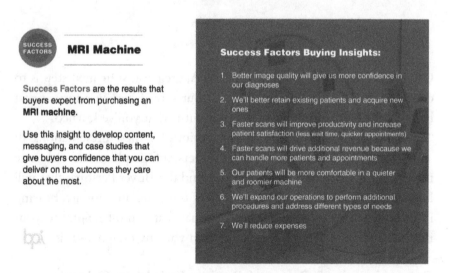

Figure 8.2   MRI machine Success Factors summary.

with the findings for Jared, the magnetic resonance imaging (MRI) machine Buyer Persona we built in Chapter 7.

The first two – Priority Initiatives (PI) and Success Factors (SF) – reveal the triggering circumstances that cause buyers to begin

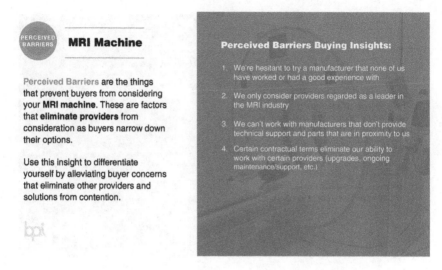

Figure 8.3   MRI machine Perceived Barriers summary.

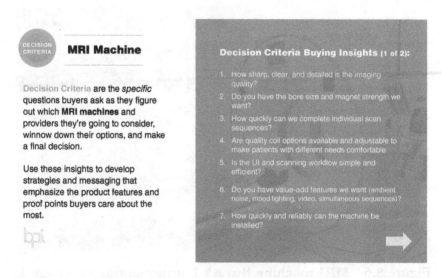

Figure 8.4   MRI machine Decision Criteria summary – page 1.

looking for a solution to a particular need that they have and the outcomes they expect from their investment.

Perceived Barriers (PB) reveal the fears and concerns that buyers have making the investment or doing so with a particular provider.

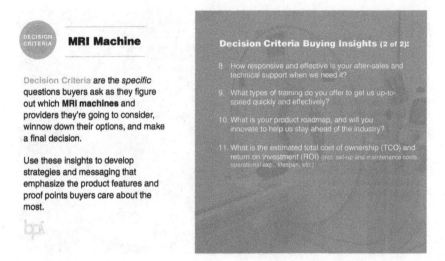

Figure 8.5   MRI machine Decision Criteria summary – page 2.

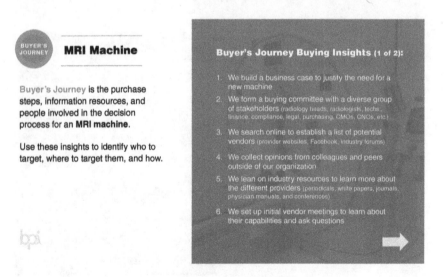

Figure 8.6   MRI machine Buyer's Journey summary – page 1.

Decision Criteria (DC) are all the questions that buyers will ask as they evaluate and winnow down their options and make a final buying decision.

Buyer's Journey identifies the individuals and roles involved in the buying committee, the steps they take to identify and evaluate their options, and the information sources they use to inform their decision.

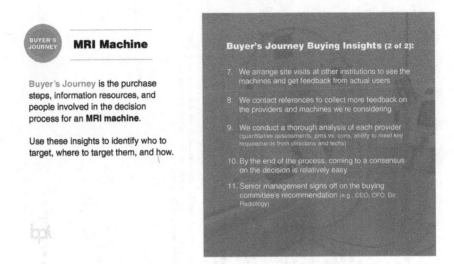

Figure 8.7   MRI machine Buyer's Journey summary – page 2.

Figures 8.8 and 8.9 are examples of how we show the verbatim quotes that support each Buying Insight that you'll pull from your Insights Aggregator spreadsheet. You will want to prioritize the insights and quotations that were expressed by multiple buyers, but since this is qualitative research, there is no hard-and-fast rule that determines how many of the people you interviewed need to have the same point of view.

Once you know which Buyer Quotes will appear in your Buyer Persona, you'll want to *slightly* edit the verbatim quotations from your interviews to make them more readable. Eliminate repeated words and half-formed phrases. But make sure not to insert your own words, sanitize the quotation, summarize salient points, or eliminate colorful turns of phrase. Your goal is to faithfully report the buyer's words, cogently communicating their thoughts and emotions, even if the sentence is a copywriter's nightmare.

Building the Buyer Profile

The Buyer Profile helps you summarize and communicate key characteristics of the buyers you interviewed to develop your Buying Insights. Most marketers give their Buyer Profiles a proper name and picture, but both are optional. It can be helpful to name the Buyer Profile, so that

PRIORITY INITIATIVES

Our current machine breaks down too much, leading to costly repairs and a burden to our patients

"The biggest issue is that we were seeing major maintenance issues resulting in machines breaking down. That downtime creates a big burden on our patients over time. If a machine isn't up at a particular time, patients can't be scanned. Recently, there were times where our staff couldn't even scan anyone. The maintenance and repair costs, as well as the cost of downtime, is unacceptable and it didn't make sense to keep the machine beyond end of life."

"The most recent need was because of downtime due to a quenched magnet that came from a leak in a facility right above us. We had to replace it. We have a busy practice, and our magnets are literally utilized 24/7. The down magnet was adjacent to our emergency department and that's where most of our ED workload occurs. We can't have magnets down in our ED. That's unacceptable."

SUCCESS FACTORS

"Our old magnets would break easily, so we would go down for a couple hours on a regular basis. The engineer would come and fix it, but it was an overall need to change out that scanner. When we have downtime like that, the workflow is affected because we have to reschedule everybody. That trickles down to patients missing appointments and it's ultimately going to delay their care, which we obviously don't want to do."

PERCEIVED BARRIERS

"It's getting hard to find replacement parts, which results in downtime. We had three or four days of downtime last month because we were trying to obtain parts. Because these parts are sitting in storage units, they degrade while they sit there. We had to have the same part replaced two or three times before we finally found one that would keep us on our feet."

DECISION CRITERIA

"Any downtime is a major problem. Every two or three months, we'd have some sort of minor repair, and we would go down for a day or two."

BUYER'S JOURNEY

Patients are complaining that they are claustrophobic or uncomfortable in our current machine

"We already had an older Company A 3T. Some of the lead techs wanted something that was more comfortable for our patients. There's a significant number of patients that were terminating scans because of claustrophobia due to the size of the bore of our scanner. MRI techs were pushing to find machines with larger bores."

"We've been having an issue due to the increase in size of our patients. The bore on the older machine isn't really wide. We aren't able to see every single patient in there. The main reason we decided we needed a new machine is to accommodate every patient, because it's uncomfortable to fit a larger patient because they are too big for our machine."

"We had a 1.5 Tesla scanner and the challenge with 1.5 Tesla scanners is that you have to use an endorectal coil. It wasn't comfortable for patients at all. We had to find a way to perform the study in a more comfortable environment without the use of that endorectal coil."

"We are having complications of getting patients into the scanner due to body size. We were having to complete scans on patients that couldn't fit into the 60-centimeter bore."

"A big part of this was to address patient claustrophobia. Americans aren't getting any smaller, everybody is getting bigger. We are in an obesity epidemic, which means we need the biggest bore possible."

Figure 8.8　MRI machine Priority Initiatives Buyer Quotes example.

PRIORITY INITIATIVES

SUCCESS FACTORS

PERCEIVED BARRIERS

DECISION CRITERIA

BUYER'S JOURNEY

How quickly can we complete individual scan sequences?

"We looked at the time for the sequences – how long it takes for each individual one. For example, for a brain MRI, Company D takes 12 minutes versus Company B who takes 14 minutes. Those small nuances and their algorithms are important. They change the timing, and it allows for different numbers of procedures to be done in a day, which plays a large role in our overall workflow."

"One of them had different scan sequences, like the smart card. It would take Company A 15-17 minutes to scan a brain, but this other provider could get it down to 12 minutes."

"When a machine can make it faster for the patient, that's important. Those scan times were pretty similar, but there were some that compress those timelines, which ultimately makes the scan go faster. As an example, a regular brain can take 12 minutes in a scanner, but if you want to make it faster, you can compress it to five minutes without compromising that image quality."

"We have to do quicker scans so we can get patients in and out faster. As we looked at the machines, we felt that Company A was better in that sense. They proved to us that they could improve our workflows and inefficiencies with this newest scanner that they offered. Their protocols allowed us to download quicker. We would have better flexibility based on radiologists' recommendations to get scans done quicker."

"Company B was better overall. We felt confident that we would be able to shorten our scan times; get more patients in, and be able to perform that MR Enterography. That way we can better see bowel scans, which requires a faster scanner. With MR Enterography, we've been able to get comparable scan times with Company A as well."

Are quality coil options available and adjustable to make patients with different needs comfortable?

"Company A's spine coil is integrated into the table, just like Company B'. The head and neck coil made great strides since the last model. We are able to adjust the head so if a patient has a humpback or are uncomfortable in the scanner, you can adjust the coil. This makes patients more comfortable in the scanner. They put a lot of effort into comfort, which is a win."

"Company A now has something called air coils. You can bend them, and they are more comfortable for a patient. If someone comes in with a broken knee, you don't have to accommodate that knee in a super tight spot. You can just wrap the knee around this coil and the patient is going to feel more comfortable. We will be able to see more patients without harming them and making them feel more comfortable."

"Company A differentiated itself with superior surface coil technology. The coils are very light and robust. Technologists love this because they're flexible. They flip on the patient easily and ultimately makes everything more comfortable for the patient."

"I look at the compatibility of the coils that are available on the market. The various coils offered are important: the neuro coil, the extremity coil, and the body coil. We wanted to make sure we had all those options available for coils so we can ensure our patients are comfortable, regardless of what type of scan they are receiving."

"There are all kinds of coils. A head coil that wraps around the head and then does its read, a breast coil, a leg and lower extremity coil, and a body coil. They all have to be compatible with the base unit and some coils are incompatible. Those coils are important."

Figure 8.9 MRI machine Decision Criteria Buyer Quotes example.

the Buyer Persona becomes "real" to internal stakeholders. Additionally, among members of a marketing team, when the Buyer Profile name is invoked in conversation, it serves as a shorthand that refers to all the Buying Insights associated with that Buyer Persona. We've seen companies use these names in internal meetings and communications whenever they want to reference the findings contained in the Buyer Persona.

There are downsides to this practice, however, as we've seen teams waste time on debates about demographics such as the age, gender, and ethnicity of their Buyer Persona when none of these will have any impact on their marketing strategies. If you think this may be a problem in your company, try to choose a name that is gender neutral and skip the photo.

Figure 8.10 shows the Buyer Profile for Jared using our MRI machine example. You may want to adjust the characteristics displayed to include any that you believe will best describe the people you include in your persona.

- **Market Segment:** Target market characteristics you identified in the design phase of the study (discussed in Chapter 4).
- **Roles and Reports To:** The roles and titles of the buyers you interviewed and who they report to. You might confirm your buyer's job title during your interviews, but whenever possible you'll want to avoid asking questions where the answers could be obtained through a quick online search. When looking for information on business-to-business (B2B) job descriptions, and background about years of experience and education, you can access data from the LinkedIn profiles of the people you interviewed.
- **Education:** The highest level of education obtained by the buyers you interviewed.
- **Solution:** The product, service, or solution your Buyer Persona is focused on.
- **Responsibilities for Decision:** A short narrative that summarizes a few key responsibilities of the buyers you interview and their most important needs and requirements for this solution purchase. You'll write this based on the Buying Insights you develop for your Buyer Persona.

Buyer Persona Profile

NAME	Jared
ROLES	Radiologist I Radiology Dept. Head Radiology / MRI Technologist I Director of IT I Program Manager
EDUCATION	BS Radiologic Technology/Science I BA Medical Diagnostic Imaging I MPH I MBA I MD I PhD

MARKET SEGMENT	Large U.S. Hospitals (100+/300+ beds) Mix of for-profit, non-profit, academic
REPORTS TO	Head of MRI Tech. I MR Team Leader I Dir., Dept. Head / Chair, VP, Imaging Services I VP of IT I CEO
SOLUTION	Closed MRI Machine

Responsibilities for Decision

I focus on streamlining our department's operations, emphasizing scheduling, scan result analysis, and staying current with MRI technology. Our previous MRI machine caused issues such as downtime, low-quality images, and patient discomfort. Upgrading our technology will enhance the patient experience, shorten scan times, boost productivity and revenue.

We partner with top MRI manufacturers for seamless integration, considering total cost of ownership. Our aim is to acquire the latest technology for exceptional image quality, patient comfort, and efficient scans.

My Top Priorities This Year

- Reading scans/diagnostics
- Treating patients/patient satisfaction
- Technical innovation and research
- Managing department/educating staff/scheduling
- Optimize workflow, efficiency, & productivity
- Grow volume/revenue
- Administration/paperwork
- Research
- Quality assurance

Resources I Trust

Internet: Manufacturer websites, physician websites, radiology forums, SCRMO, Facebook groups

Industry: White papers, events/conferences (RSNA), Publications (Physicians manuals, TTN, ICE - Advancing Imaging Professional)

Peers/Word of mouth: Industry peers, internal co-workers, customer references, University organizations

Internal: C-Suite, Radiologists, other physicians, IT, MRI Techs, Purchasing/Supply Chain, Operations, Compliance, Legal, Administrative, Finance

Figure 8.10 MRI machine Buyer Profile.

- **My Top Priorities This Year:** If you have time at the end of your interviews, try to ask buyers for their top two to three priorities over the next year. They may identify certain things that have nothing to do with the buying decision you are focused on, and that's okay. It's nice to add this to your Buyer Profile to provide a high-level perspective of other things that are on the minds of buyers.
- **Resources I Trust:** A summary of the different sources your buyers will identify throughout the interview that they used to inform their buying decision. This information will come directly from your interviews, but feel free to supplement your interview findings with any data from other sources that you trust.

If you want to capture any other profile information during your interviews, reserve any such questions for the end of the interview. As we discussed in Chapter 6, you should aim to engage your buyer in telling their story as soon as possible in order to set the tone for a conversation that enlists their full attention. Keep any questions that are unrelated to the buyer's story to a bare minimum and ask them only after you have learned everything you can about the decision.

You may have information from other sources including social media and generative AI (GenAI) that will help you complete the Buyer Profile. Just keep in mind that every characteristic you add to your Buyer Profile should help you make better marketing decisions. Irrelevant information puts your Buyer Persona initiative at risk with stakeholders who may view it as foolish or question the need for additional personas. You should keep your focus on the Buying Insights and ensure that the Buyer Profile is used to help your team identify people who share your Buyer Persona's expectations.

Identify Top Themes That Will Resonate with Buyers

After working in your Insights Aggregator spreadsheet, writing headlines, selecting quotes, and creating your Buyer Persona, something is likely happening whether you intended it to or not: you are starting to *internalize your buyer's story*. Rather than observing their mindset from a distance, you're now in the front row. You intuitively know what buyers care about most, what their top concerns are, and what they need to achieve through this purchase to deem it successful. You're feeling this because you have listened to them carefully, read back the transcripts from your interviews, and immersed yourself in their mindset and the steps they took in their buying journey.

Rather than putting this newfound knowledge on the shelf, the final step to developing your Buyer Persona is summarizing the main things that buyers need to know to feel confident and assured in their buying decision. These are the themes you can feel confident will resonate with buyers the most as they look for a solution to a need they have and evaluate their options.

The way you'll do this is to look *across* the first four Rings of Buying Insight – Priority Initiatives, Success Factors, Perceived Barriers, and Decision Criteria – to identify buyer goals, concerns, and questions that connect with a more central buyer need. These higher-order needs are typically linked to multiple insights within the first four Rings and have particular importance to buyers. There is no rule about how many you should come up with, but we typically discover five to eight per Buyer Persona.

Let's look at our MRI machine example again. For this study, we identified a total of 28 insights across the first four Rings of Buying Insight (only excluding Buyer's Journey). From these 28 insights, we identified 6 primary needs, or themes, that rise above the rest in terms of their importance to buyers. Here's the six and how we came up with each:

- **Reduce Scan Times:** in our interviews, MRI machine buyers pointed to several features that enable faster scan times (stronger magnet, intuitive user interface [UI], efficient workflows) *plus* important outcomes they expect from doing so (improving patient satisfaction, retention, revenue, and productivity).
- **Produce Sharper and Clearer Images:** by improving image quality, buyers told us they can achieve two out of the seven outcomes (Success Factors) that they care about most (improve confidence in patient diagnosis and growing the practice).

- **Improve a Patient's Comfort and Appointment Experience:** this came up repeatedly as an important outcome of the purchase (Success Factors). Buyers also pointed out several machine features they were looking for to improve the patient experience (larger bore hole, adjustable coils, ambient noise, mood lighting, and video).
- **Get Up and Running Quickly:** buyers identified several things that give them confidence they can get a new MRI machine installed and operating quickly (access to workflow and technology experts, comprehensive training, local support, and parts).
- **Future-proof Operations with Reliable Technology and Continuous Innovation:** replacing their old and archaic MRI machine is a top trigger for this purchase (Priority Initiatives) and buyers want to know the manufacturer will continue to innovate so they can grow and evolve with them in the future.
- **Partner with an Established Leader in Imaging Technology and Operations:** because an MRI machine is fundamental to the hospital's imaging capabilities and a significant capital investment, buyers are looking for indications that this is an established manufacturer that they can trust (which can be evidenced by a manufacturer's client base, references, awards, research focus and investments, etc.).

In Figures 8.11 and 8.12 you'll see how we typically include these themes in a Buyer Persona. For each of these six themes, there are several insights that link to each one and we reference back to them by annotating the insight with its respective Ring of Buying Insight (PI = Priority Initiatives, SF = Success Factors, PB = Perceived Barriers, and DC = Decision Criteria).

Although there is an art and a science to coming up with these top themes, once you immerse yourself in the interviews and build your Buyer Persona, you'll see that they usually reveal themselves quite clearly. As a litmus test, after you've identified the top themes, read through all of them and if you get the sense that they accurately capture the *primary expectations* you heard from buyers, then you've done your job well. If

Message Themes That Will Resonate with MRI Machine Buyers*

Based on analysis across the 5 Rings of Buying Insight™

1. **Reduce Scan Times**
   - A stronger magnet, intuitive UI, and efficient workflows enables faster scan sequences [PI, SF, DC]
   - Improve patient satisfaction and retention with shorter appointments and less time in the machine [SF]
   - Increase revenue by handling more patients and appointments [SF]
   - Improve productivity of clinicians, image technologists, and office staff [SF]

2. **Produce Sharper and Clearer Images**
   - Improve confidence in your diagnosis [SF]
   - Grow the practice by handling additional procedures enabled by higher-resolution imaging [SF]

3. **Improve a Patient's Comfort and Appointment Experience**
   - Faster scans get patients in-and-out of appointments and the machine more quickly [SF]
   - A larger bore/hole enables patients to fit in the machine more comfortably [PI, DC]
   - Adjustable coil options ensure patients with different needs and ailments will be comfortable [DC]
   - Additional features improve the experience inside the machine – ambient noise, mood lighting, video [DC]

Figure 8.11 MRI machine message themes that will resonate with buyers – page 1.

Message Themes That Will Resonate with MRI Machine Buyers*

Based on analysis across the 5 Rings of Buying Insight™

4. Get Up and Running Quickly

- Access to workflow and technology experts that get your machine installed quickly and effectively [DC]
- Comprehensive training options to get clinicians, technicians, and support staff up-to-speed rapidly [DC]
- Local access to expert after-sale technical support and parts so you stay up-and-running [PB]

5. Future-proof Operations with Reliable Technology and Continuous Innovation

- Replace your older machine with the latest in imaging technology and upgrade options [PI]
- Reduce machine breakdowns that cause patient frustration and costly repairs [PI]
- Partner with a manufacturer committed to delivering best-in-class imaging technology now and in the future [DC]

6. Partner with an Established Leader in Imaging Technology and Operations [PB]

- [Depends on manufacturer – could include things like client base information/statistics/references, awards and achievements, research focus and investments, future plans, etc.]

Figure 8.12   MRI machine message themes that will resonate with buyers – page 2.

you get the sense that something is missing, go back and identify the gap. Because you have internalized your buyer's story, this shouldn't be too hard because the nagging feeling that you missed something important will typically draw you like a magnet to the very thing that gave you that feeling in the first place.

Summary

In this chapter, we covered the following points:

- There are several ways to communicate Buying Insights for your Buyer Persona including presentation slides (Power-Point, Google Slides, Prezi, and others), posters, info-graphics, and intranet sites. All are appropriate depending on your organization's needs and how they best digest information. Choose a format that is most helpful to your internal audience.
- Whichever format you choose, include a summary of the Buying Insights for each of the 5 Rings of Buying Insight plus Buyer Quotes that support each. You'll pull these from your Insights Aggregator spreadsheet.
- Add a Buyer Profile that summarizes the key characteristics of the buyers you interviewed to develop your Buying Insights – Market Segment, Role, Reports To, Education, Solution, Responsibilities for Decision, My Top Priorities This Year, and Resources I Trust are great ones to start with.
- Identify and summarize the top five to eight buyer needs, or themes, from the first four Rings of Buying Insight. These are the themes you can feel confident will resonate with buyers the most as they look for a solution and evaluate their options.

9 | Conduct Survey Research to Enhance Buying Insights

We are often asked about the value of conducting survey research to validate and enhance Buying Insights developed from one-on-one interviews. Survey research typically includes more structured questions (e.g. ratings, rankings, select from a list of choices, etc.) with a larger number of buyers. The thinking is logical – by collecting more information from buyers, you'll increase the confidence you have in your Buyer Persona and develop additional insights to make even better decisions about how to market and sell to them.

Ways to Enhance Your Buyer Persona with Survey Research

Based on the hundreds of studies we've been involved in, there has never been an instance where survey research invalidated what we learned from the initial, one-on-one buyer interviews. In fact, the opposite is true – survey research always validates what we have learned and increases the confidence in the findings.

147

However, survey research will greatly *enhance* your Buyer Persona in several important ways, including:

- **Confirming the accuracy and validity of your Buyer Persona:** There may be times where you need to collect data from additional buyers to help bolster your internal stakeholders' confidence in the insights from your one-on-one interviews even more (and that's okay). Survey research is the perfect tool to accomplish this.

- **Determining which buyer expectations are most important in the buying decision:** Doing so will help you prioritize your marketing activities and resources, so they're focused on the things that matter most to buyers.

- **Testing value proposition and market messages:** Developing and refreshing your messaging is one of the first things most organizations do after developing their Buyer Persona (more on this in Chapter 10). Survey research enables you to test these messages with buyers and fine-tune them for greater impact.

- **Identifying and understanding buyer segments:** Survey research will reveal whether it's beneficial to tailor your marketing strategies to different segments of the market (e.g. by company size, industry, geography, buyer role, etc.) or stick with one consistent approach across all of them.

None of these areas is a must; you have the flexibility to focus a survey on whatever Buying Insights you think would be the most worthwhile. However, in our experience, these are the areas that provide the most useful learnings because they bolster stakeholder confidence in your Buyer Persona and provide additional Buying Insights that enable you to market and sell to your buyers even more effectively.

For the remainder of this chapter, we'll cover each of these areas in more detail. Although getting into specific survey questions and statistical methods is beyond the scope of this book, we have provided enough detail for you to confidently get started on your own survey or work with a third-party research firm to assist you. We close out the chapter with some guidance on the types of buyers you should survey because who you interview is just as important as what you ask them.

Confirm the Accuracy and Validity of Your Buyer Persona

One of the benefits of conducting a survey with a larger number of buyers is that it will give you even more confidence that the buyer expectations you identified from your one-on-one interviews are accurate and representative of the markets you're targeting. There are various ways to achieve this in a survey, but we have found that asking buyers a mix of closed-ended questions (e.g. ratings, rankings, select from a list of choices, etc.) and open-ended questions (free-form responses) does the job well. You can do this for each of the 5 Rings of Buying Insight or pick-and-choose if there are certain insights you're more focused on than others.

For example, let's take the Success Factors we identified in our magnetic resonance imaging (MRI) machine Buyer Persona. Here are the types of survey questions you can use to further confirm that each Success Factor is important to buyers:

Q1. In the space below, please indicate all the important outcomes or benefits you are expecting from this MRI machine purchase.

_____

_____

Q2. On a 10-point scale, where "1" is "Not at All Important" and "10" is "Very Important," to what extent is each of the items in Figure 9.1 an important outcome that you need from a new MRI machine? *(Rate Each)*

Q1 is an open-ended question where buyers have the opportunity to speak (if a phone survey) or type in (if an online survey) their response. Q2 is a closed-ended question where buyers will rate each of the seven Success Factors from the Buyer Persona on a 10-point scale.

Asking Q1 as an open-ended question first eliminates the risk that buyers will be influenced (or biased) by any of the Success Factors listed in Q2. They will respond freely and feel unencumbered by anything that

	Not at All Important									Very Important
	1	2	3	4	5	6	7	8	9	10
1. Better image quality will give us more confidence in our diagnosis	O	O	O	O	O	O	O	O	O	O
2. We'll better retain existing patients and acquire new ones	O	O	O	O	O	O	O	O	O	O
3. Faster scans will improve productivity and increase patient satisfaction	O	O	O	O	O	O	O	O	O	O
4. Faster scans will drive additional revenue because we can handle more patients and appointments	O	O	O	O	O	O	O	O	O	O
5. Our patients will be more comfortable in a quieter and roomier machine	O	O	O	O	O	O	O	O	O	O
6. We'll expand our operations to perform additional procedures and address different types of needs	O	O	O	O	O	O	O	O	O	O
7. We'll reduce expenses	O	O	O	O	O	O	O	O	O	O

Figure 9.1 Example question to determine Success Factors importance.

might inadvertently put an idea in their head that they didn't think of on their own. After you've collected all the responses to Q1, compare the results to the Success Factors from the Buyer Persona to determine if they are the same (a confirmational finding) or if there are any new ones you want to add to it (an additional finding).

By asking Q2, you'll also get direct input on each of the seven Success Factors. Since these were identified from the one-on-one interviews, there is a strong likelihood that all or most will be regarded as important to buyers, but this is the opportunity to validate that assumption.

Similar survey approaches can be taken for each of the 5 Rings of Buying Insight, including Buyer's Journey. For example, one of the questions that marketers often ask is where they can best reach buyers across the myriad of places they might go to educate themselves about a particular solution and their options. Your one-on-one interviews will reveal these sources, but a survey is a great opportunity to validate what you learned and identify additional information sources that buyers use.

Determine Which Buyer Expectations Are the Most Important

Not all buyer expectations are created equal – there are assuredly some that are more important than others. If the analysis of your one-on-one interview transcripts reveals a buyer expectation you include in your Buyer Persona, you should feel confident that it is important. However, only survey research, where you have the opportunity to collect input from a larger number of buyers, can reliably tell you which buyer expectations are the most (and least important) in their buying decision. This is often referred to as "relative importance" since the importance of something is considered *relative* to something else.

For example, in the case of the MRI machine Buyer Persona, we identified 11 Decision Criteria (Figures 8.4 and 8.5). If you're an MRI machine manufacturer, you should develop strategies to address each of these questions since buyers use them to evaluate the options they're considering, and each is likely to come up at some point in their buying journey. However, it's also reasonable for you to ask which of the 11 Decision Criteria are the most important to buyers. Knowing this would help you prioritize your marketing activities, messages, and resources.

Survey research is the perfect tool to assess the relative importance between the buyer expectations identified in your Buyer Persona. Using our MRI machine Buyer Persona, here are four different ways to determine the relative importance of the 11 Decision Criteria (from the least to most sophisticated approach):

- **Select Top 1 or 2:** Have buyers select the top 1 or 2 Decision Criteria that are the *most* important in their buying decision out of the 11. It's also useful to ask buyers which one or two are the *least* important and report on those results as well.
- **Rankings:** Have buyers rank the 11 MRI machine Decision Criteria from 1 (most important) to 11 (least important).
- **Chip Allocation:** Have buyers allocate 100 "chips" (or points) across the 11 Decision Criteria. The more chips a buyer allocates to a Decision Criteria, the more important it is. You can allocate as many or as few chips as you want to each of the 11 Decision Criteria.

- **Choice-based Exercise** (such as *Maximum Difference Scaling*): Have buyers go through a series of questions – like the one in Figure 9.2 – where they indicate which Decision Criteria is the MOST important in their buying decision and which is the LEAST important. Using this approach, buyers answer a series of questions where 4 of the 11 Decision Criteria randomly appear on the screen (in the case of an online survey). The survey will continue to ask and collect which is the MOST and LEAST important. You can typically gather all the survey data you need by having buyers answer four to six questions just like this (one after another) where the four options vary randomly from question to question.

From a methodology standpoint, *Select Top 1 or 2* and *Rankings* are the most straightforward to use and will give you a good sense of which Decision Criteria are the most and least important. These approaches won't tell you how much more important one Decision Criteria is relative to another, but they will provide a hierarchical order (e.g. which Decision Criteria is the most important, second most important, third most important, and so on).

Of the following, which is the MOST important and which is the LEAST important in terms of which MRI machine your hospital will purchase?	MOST Important	LEAST Important
Image quality (sharp, clear, detailed)	O	O
The speed of scan sequences	O	O
How quickly the machine can be installed	O	O
Responsive and effective after-sale technical support	O	O

Figure 9.2 Example choice-based question to determine Decision Criteria importance.

For example, Figure 9.3 shows you what the results from a *Rankings* exercise might look like for the MRI machine Decision Criteria. The chart reveals the percentage of time a buyer ranked each Decision Criteria as the first or second most important in their buying decision. These results don't mean that you should ignore *training to get us up-to-speed quickly and effectively* in your marketing efforts or focus all your resources on *sharp, clear, and detailed imaging quality* – both are important – but it does provide more guidance in terms of how you might prioritize them.

The *Chip Allocation* and *Choice-based* approaches (in particular), require a bit more analytical sophistication to use, but have the advantage of revealing the importance of buyer expectations both hierarchically and by order of magnitude (how much more important one Decision Criteria is versus another).

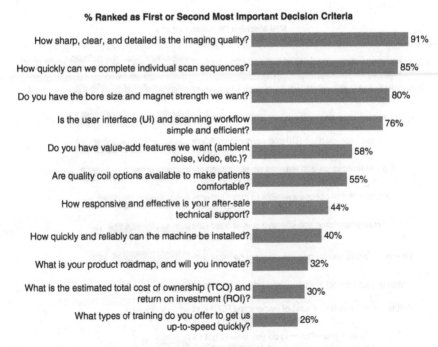

% Ranked as First or Second Most Important Decision Criteria

Decision Criteria	%
How sharp, clear, and detailed is the imaging quality?	91%
How quickly can we complete individual scan sequences?	85%
Do you have the bore size and magnet strength we want?	80%
Is the user interface (UI) and scanning workflow simple and efficient?	76%
Do you have value-add features we want (ambient noise, video, etc.)?	58%
Are quality coil options available to make patients comfortable?	55%
How responsive and effective is your after-sale technical support?	44%
How quickly and reliably can the machine be installed?	40%
What is your product roadmap, and will you innovate?	32%
What is the estimated total cost of ownership (TCO) and return on investment (ROI)?	30%
What types of training do you offer to get us up-to-speed quickly?	26%

Figure 9.3   Example results for MRI machine Decision Criteria ranking.

Figure 9.4 shows you what the results from a *Chip Allocation* exercise might look like for the MRI machine Decision Criteria. In this example, we're showing the average number of chips buyers allocated to each Decision Criteria (with the maximum number being 100). The more chips allocated to a particular Decision Criteria, the more important it is to buyers in their buying decision. Because this is an allocation exercise it also reveals how important individual Decision Criteria are in relation to one another. In this example, because *sharp, clear, and detailed imaging quality* is two times higher than *how quickly and reliably the machine can be installed,* you can conclude that it's two times more important in the buying decision.

Because more advanced statistical analysis is required to analyze the survey data from a *Choice-based* approach, you should consult with your in-house market research team or a third-party research firm to assist you.

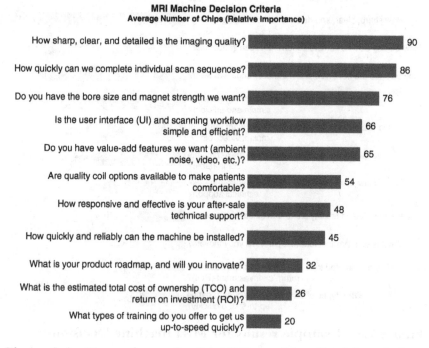

MRI Machine Decision Criteria
Average Number of Chips (Relative Importance)

Decision Criteria	Chips
How sharp, clear, and detailed is the imaging quality?	90
How quickly can we complete individual scan sequences?	86
Do you have the bore size and magnet strength we want?	76
Is the user interface (UI) and scanning workflow simple and efficient?	66
Do you have value-add features we want (ambient noise, video, etc.)?	65
Are quality coil options available to make patients comfortable?	54
How responsive and effective is your after-sale technical support?	48
How quickly and reliably can the machine be installed?	45
What is your product roadmap, and will you innovate?	32
What is the estimated total cost of ownership (TCO) and return on investment (ROI)?	26
What types of training do you offer to get us up-to-speed quickly?	20

Figure 9.4　Example results for MRI machine Decision Criteria chip allocation.

Test Value Proposition and Market Messaging Concepts

Once you complete your Buyer Persona, you will have insights that reveal everything prospective buyers want to know and experience in order to have confidence buying from you. As you will see in Chapter 10, you can use this knowledge to develop messages that resonate with buyers by aligning them to their most important needs and your company's unique capabilities. Once you develop the messages, survey research provides a great opportunity to test them with prospective buyers before you start using them in the market. By doing so, you will identify which messages influence buyers the most and gain additional insights to fine-tune them for success.

Let's stick with our MRI machine example. Based on the Buyer Persona, you would likely focus some of your messaging on *reducing scan times* since this was identified as a critical buyer need. Here are four message alternatives that you might develop:

- In an independent study, our MRI machine produced images that are at least two times faster than any other machine on the market.
- By reducing scan times, you will improve patient satisfaction and increase the number of appointments you can handle on a daily basis.
- Our 3.0 Tesla magnet, intuitive user interface (UI), and efficient workflows enable you to get patients in and out of appointments more quickly.
- Faster imaging sequences will improve the productivity of your clinicians and image technicians.

Based on the Buyer Persona insights, it's reasonable to expect that any of these messages would resonate with prospective MRI machine buyers. However, without further testing, there is no way to know which will influence buyers the most. If an A/B test isn't possible – where you test to see which message alternatives perform better in an in-market experiment (such as on a website) – the next best alternative is survey research.

Here are a few ways to accomplish this in your survey:

- **Ratings:** Have buyers rate each message alternative on a 10-point scale for things such as:
  - Clarity – how clear and well understood the message is.
  - Relevance – how well the message aligns with buyer needs.
  - Differentiation – how different or unique the message is.
  - Compelling – to what extent the message sparks a buyer's interest in your solution.

- **Select the Top Message:** From a set of messages, have buyers select the one that is the most important (or influential) in their buying decision.
- **Ranking:** From a set of messages, have buyers rank each of them from most to least important in their buying decision.
- **Choice-based Exercise** (such as *Maximum Difference Scaling*): Described earlier in this chapter, this approach is perfectly suited to test message concepts because buyers select which is the MOST important and the LEAST important in their buying decision. The survey data enables you to determine importance both hierarchically (which message is the most important, second most important, third most important, and so on) and by order of magnitude (how much more important is one message versus another). As mentioned earlier, this approach does require more survey and analytic sophistication, but it's a great option if you have the internal know-how or can partner with a third-party research firm to assist you.

Regardless of which approach you use, survey research is a great tool to test your messages with prospective buyers to ensure that they are having the desired impact on their buying decision.

Identify and Understand Buyer Segments

As we've discussed throughout this book, when it comes to high-consideration buying decisions, it's imperative to understand buyer expectations across the entire buying committee. For these types of decisions, when the buying center searches for alternatives, winnows down their options, and makes a buying decision, you want to understand the mindset of the collective decision influencers involved. This is the core of your Buyer Persona and what the 5 Rings of Buying Insight reveal.

However, there are times when important differences in buyer expectations may exist across different "segments" of the market – such as by company size, industry, geography, or a buyer's role.

For example, if an MRI machine manufacturer targets both large hospitals and smaller independent imaging practices, it's conceivable that some of the needs, expectations, and aspects of the buying journey could vary across these two cohorts. If you suspect that this is the case, it's appropriate to do a deeper exploration of each of these segments in your survey. Doing so will confirm or refute your suspicions and provide the Buying Insights you need to tailor your marketing approach if you decide to do so.

As with most things related to survey research, there are different approaches to achieving a particular objective – in this case, identifying any meaningful differences in buyer expectations across different segments of your market. Fortunately, the approach we recommend is straightforward, doesn't require any major modifications to your survey, and will do the job well. Here are the three steps you can take:

1. Complete enough survey interviews in *each* segment so a reliable evaluation can be made between them. If you're working with your in-house market research team or a third-party research firm, they can help you determine how many completed surveys are enough, but the important thing is to design the study so you have a sufficient number in each segment to analyze the results within them.

2. Complete a thorough side-by-side comparison of results between the segments in your study. This should be done across buyer expectations for each of the 5 Rings of Buying Insight.

3. Based on this comparison, and your own capabilities, decide whether or not it's worthwhile to tailor your marketing and sales approach within certain market segments.

The first two steps are highly objective. They simply require you to make some conscious decisions about the number of surveys you complete in each market segment and then compare the results across them. Figure 9.5 shows you what the results from a chip allocation exercise might look like for the MRI machine Decision Criteria between two markets – *Large Hospitals* and *Small Independent Medical Imaging Practices*. In this example, there are very few differences across 8 of the 11 Decision Criteria, but significant differences among three of them.

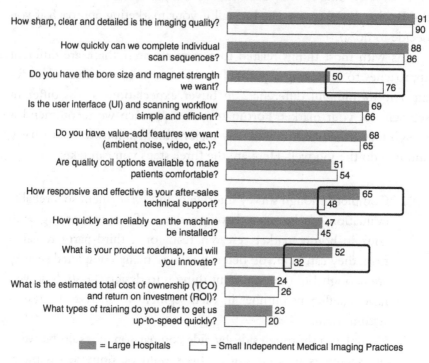

Figure 9.5   Example of segmented results for MRI machine Decision Criteria chip allocation.

For the third step, you will want to consider if the differences you discovered between the segments are relevant to your ability to persuade these buyers. Using the MRI machine example, you can do this by building a table like the one in Figure 9.6 that reflects each of the 39 Buying Insights from your spreadsheet. The headlines with an "X" in the Large Hospital column are more exclusive to large hospitals and those with an "X" in the Smaller Imaging Practices column are more exclusive to that segment of buyers. Significantly, there are 30 Buying Insights, with an "X" that apply to both audiences.

If your company has a compelling way to address any of the five insights that are exclusive to Large Hospitals, or any of the four that are unique to Smaller Imaging Practices, you have evidence that tailoring your marketing approach will help you to win more business. But if the most compelling aspect of your story aligns with the 30 Buying Insights that Large Hospitals and Smaller Imaging Practices have in common, you would be better off with one consistent approach across both segments.

Who Should You Survey?

Once you've determined the key areas you want to cover in your survey, the next step is to define *who* it is you're actually going to survey. Like the one-on-one interviews, you'll want to define specific characteristics of the buyers you're going to target such as company size, country, industry, role within the company, etc. Once again, you have complete discretion to define these characteristics however you wish. The important thing is to define them, so they reflect the markets and buyers you are most interested in gaining additional Buying Insights for.

If the sole or primary goal of the survey is to validate the Buying Insights from your Buyer Persona and learn even more about this target market, then the characteristics should be the same as those you used for the one-on-one interviews (see Chapter 4).

If, on the other hand, you're trying to determine if the Buying Insights are consistent or vary at all in other markets, then you'll want to adjust them, so they reflect these new (or additional) targets.

5 Rings	Buying Insights	Large Hospitals	Small Independents
Priority Initiatives	We are having trouble diagnosing patients because of poor image quality in our current machine	X	X
	Our current machine is archaic and too slow	X	X
	Our current machine breaks down too much, leading to costly repairs and a burden to our patients	X	X
	Patients are complaining that they are claustrophobic or uncomfortable in our current machine	X	X
	We're losing revenue because of bad patient reviews, limited machine availability, and long wait times	**X**	
	Our facility is expanding, and we need a new machine to accommodate that growth		**X**
Success Factors	Better image quality will give us more confidence in our diagnoses	X	X
	We'll better retain existing patients and acquire new ones	**X**	X
	Faster scans will improve productivity and increase patient satisfaction (less wait time, quicker appointments)	X	X
	Faster scans will drive additional revenue because we can handle more patients and appointments	**X**	**X**
	Our patients will be more comfortable in a quieter and roomier machine	X	X
	We'll expand our operations to perform additional procedures and address different types of needs		**X**
	We'll reduce expenses	X	X

Figure 9.6   Example of segmented analysis for MRI machine Buying Insights.

5 Rings	Buying Insights	Large Hospitals	Small Independents
Perceived Barriers	We're hesitant to try a manufacturer that none of us have worked or had a good experience with	X	X
	We only consider providers regarded as leaders in the MRI industry	X	X
	We can't work with manufacturers that don't provide technical support and parts that are in proximity to us	X	X
	Certain contractual terms eliminate our ability to work with certain providers (upgrades, ongoing maintenance/support, etc.)	**X**	
Decision Criteria	How sharp, clear, and detailed is the imaging quality?	X	X
	Do you have the bore size and magnet strength we want?	X	X
	How quickly can we complete individual scan sequences?	X	**X**
	Are quality coil options available and adjustable to make patients with different needs comfortable?	X	X
	Is the user interface (UI) and scanning workflow simple and efficient?	X	X
	Do you have value-add features we want (ambient noise, mood lighting, video, simultaneous sequences)?	X	X
	How quickly and reliably can the machine be installed?	**X**	
	How responsive and effective is your after-sale, technical support when we need it?	X	X
	What types of training do you offer to get us up-to-speed quickly and effectively?	**X**	
	What is your product roadmap, and will you innovate to help us stay ahead of the industry?	X	X
	What is the estimated total cost of ownership (TCO) and return on investment (ROI) (incl. set-up and maintenance costs, operational exp., lifespan, etc.)?	X	X

Figure 9.6 (*Continued*)

5 Rings	Buying Insights	Large Hospitals	Small Independents
Buyer's Journey	We build a business case to justify the need for a new machine	X	X
	We form a buying committee with a diverse group of stakeholders (radiology heads, radiologists, techs., finance, compliance, legal, purchasing, CMOs, CNOs, etc.)	X	X
	We search online to establish a list of potential vendors (provider websites, Facebook, industry forums)	X	X
	We collect opinions from colleagues and peers outside of our organization	X	X
	We lean on industry resources to learn more about the different providers (periodicals, white papers, journals, physician manuals, and conferences)	X	X
	We set up initial vendor meetings to learn about their capabilities and ask questions	X	X
	We arrange site visits at other institutions to see the machines and get feedback from actual users	X	X
	We contact references to collect more feedback on the providers and machines we're considering	X	X
	We conduct a thorough analysis of each provider (quantitative assessments, pros vs. cons, ability to meet key requirements from clinicians and techs)	X	X
	By the end of the process, coming to a consensus on the decision is relatively easy	X	X
	Senior management signs off on the buying committee's recommendation (e.g., CEO, CFO, Dir. Radiology)	X	X

Figure 9.6 *(Continued)*

Note that it's not uncommon to want to accomplish both objectives. For example, to develop the MRI machine Buyer Persona, we initially conducted interviews with buyers in large U.S. hospitals. If an MRI manufacturer wanted to validate this persona (focused on large U.S. hospitals) *plus* test to see if the Buying Insights vary at all in European countries, they'd simply conduct enough surveys in both geographies to analyze the results within each.

Surveying Recent Buyers and Prospective Buyers

The other study design question you'll need to decide on is whether to survey *recent buyers* only or include *prospective buyers* in your survey as well.

As we defined them in Chapter 3, *recent buyers* are buyers that have made the exact same buying decision within the last three to six months that you're trying to influence. These types of buyers were the sole focus of the one-on-one interviews you used to create your Buyer Persona to ensure that anyone you interviewed was speaking about an actual buying decision in which they were involved. Recall that one of the primary reasons for building a Buyer Persona is to take all the guesswork out of marketing. You can only do that by interviewing buyers that have recently been through a buying decision so they can tell you their mindset and the actual steps they took throughout their buying journey.

For a survey, where you need to interview a larger number of buyers, you may need to expand your target to also include *prospective buyers*. Whereas recent buyers recently made the same type of buying decision you're trying to influence, prospective buyers haven't, but there are indicators that they will in the near future.

The reason for expanding the audience is that there may not be enough recent buyers in the market to complete as many survey interviews as you need. If the buying decision has a large market and isn't a new solution category, then you may be able to interview recent buyers exclusively. If it's a smaller market, or a newer solution category, you'll likely need to survey recent buyers *and* prospective buyers to complete enough survey interviews for statistically reliable results, and that's certainly a sound approach.

There are a few ways to identify prospective buyers in the early part of your survey. The most direct way – and the way we recommend – is to simply ask them how likely they are to look for a particular solution in the next 6–12 months.

For example, if we were doing a survey for the MRI machine, we would ask: "How likely are you to purchase a new MRI machine in the next 6 months?" Survey respondents can answer "very likely," "somewhat likely," or "not likely."

- Those that indicate they are "very likely" will be classified as a prospective buyer and included in the survey.
- Those that answer "somewhat likely" or "not likely" are excluded because they don't have an imminent need and are much less likely to give you thoughtful survey answers. Note: If you are really struggling to find enough prospective buyers for your survey, you can consider accepting those that answer "somewhat likely," but our recommendation is to reject those respondents unless absolutely needed.

Summary

In this chapter, we covered the following points:

- After completing your Buyer Persona, conducting a survey with a larger number of buyers can enhance your research by:
  - Confirming the accuracy and validity of your Buyer Persona – will help bolster your internal stakeholders' confidence in the Buying Insights.
  - Determining which buyer expectations are most important in the buying decision – will help you to prioritize your marketing activities, messaging, and resources.
  - Testing value proposition and marketing messages – allows you to evaluate message alternatives with buyers and fine-tune them for greater impact.

- Identifying and understanding buyer segments – will help you determine whether it's beneficial to tailor your marketing strategies to different segments of the market or stick with one consistent approach.
- Survey buyers that reflect where you need additional Buying Insights the most:
  - If the sole or primary purpose of the survey is to validate your Buyer Persona, use the same buyer specifications that you used for your one-on-one interviews.
  - If you want to gain insights in new or additional markets, adjust the characteristics of buyers you're targeting in the survey accordingly.
- In addition to *recent buyers*, consider surveying *prospective buyers* in order to complete enough interviews for statistically reliable results.

PART
IV

Aligning Your Strategies to Win More Business

Now that you understand the attributes of useful Buyer Personas and the methodology to discover Buying Insights, we want to be sure you have a clear plan to use your insights to guide your marketing decisions. Your Buyer Personas are a marketing tool – a means and not an end. We hear from marketers every day who are responding to a directive to build Buyer Personas, but they can't tell us how they will be used.

Harold Geneen, the twentieth century business executive who *The New York Times* compared to General George S. Patton, Alexander the Great, and Napoleon, reflected on strategy with these words: "You read a book from beginning to end. You run a business the opposite way. You start with the end, and then you do everything you must to reach it."

We built the Buyer Persona methodology because we knew precisely what the end result needed to be. Our vision didn't begin with the goal to invent a new research methodology or to understand buyers. Instead, we realized that marketers of high-consideration products needed the insight and confidence to build strategies that would help buyers choose their solution. So, we invented a methodology that would provide it.

In this final part of the book, we'll show you different ways to use your Buyer Persona to make decisions and execute strategies that will help you to win more business. Chapter 10 includes a step-by-step approach to using Buyer Persona insights to develop compelling marketing messages that meet at the intersection of what buyers want and what your organization wants to say. In Chapter 11, we'll reveal different ways to use each of the 5 Rings of Buying Insight to develop strategies, content, and experiences that increase a buyer's confidence in your capabilities. Finally, in Chapter 12, we'll consider the implications that Buyer Personas suggest for changing the way business is conducted going forward, as organizations incorporate the voice of the buyer into many crucial decisions – and as marketing gains new, respected authority.

10

Decide What to Say to Buyers

A few years back, Linda Stone, a former Apple and Microsoft executive, coined the term *continuous partial attention* (CPA) to describe an increasingly pervasive mental state unique to the digital age. Stone defined CPA as the state of mind that people experience as they try to pay attention to multiple sources of information. The desire to optimize opportunities and maintain human connections has always been a fundamental aspect of humanity, but our "always on, anywhere, anytime" environment has ratcheted up the stakes.

Catching someone's attention and being heard amid this streaming torrent of information is the greatest challenge of contemporary marketing. The buyers we need to persuade are navigating an overwhelming flood of information, rapidly processing and eliminating anything that doesn't instantly connect with their priorities and expectations. That ever-present "x" button is our biggest threat as buyers quickly delete any e-mail and close any document that doesn't tell them something that clearly delivers value.

169

Will Your Current Approach Work?

Against this backdrop we can begin to see the futility of traditional approaches for choosing the words and topics that engage buyers. Whether selecting themes for an important campaign, preparing for an upcoming launch, or planning for a major event, those who are trying to influence buyers are probably quite knowledgeable about the value delivered by your product or service, as well as your company's goals.

Working alone or in a meeting with these experts, such initiatives often begin by concentrating on the people you want to influence, imagining their goals, and focusing on statements describing the benefits of your approach. Product experts tend to explain how the new functionality will help companies to grow their business, increase operational efficiency, or reduce costs. An expert on the competition may contribute points about why your solution is superior. Someone else describes the need to educate buyers about your company's vision to address an emerging market trend.

This approach to message development is so commonplace that marketers don't notice that they are attempting to build buyer-focused messaging in a setting where the buyer's perspective is unrepresented. Sure, everyone is thinking about the buyer as they convert features to benefits, focusing on the results your solution delivers rather than its capabilities. But it's unlikely that anyone participating in this exercise can say, for example, that your buyer already knows that a new magnetic resonance imaging (MRI) machine will break down less than their current machine. Will anyone have the confidence to inform the meeting that the head of radiology is far more interested in hearing about your MRI machine's magnet strength relative to other brands and models in the market? And who can defend the need for this specificity when the detractors note that this is a feature, and that the message must instead focus on the benefit of better image quality.

Your messaging decisions must take into account your company's goal to communicate the value of its solutions as well as your buyer's attitudes, needs, and concerns. Through the lens of the 5 Rings of

Buying Insight, you have a tool to bring your buyer's authentic voice to bear on the messaging decision.

In their interviews, your buyers described their Priority Initiatives or the business triggers that caused them to abandon the status quo and become interested in investing in a solution. Their Success Factors described the benefits that motivated this investment. You know about the negative perceptions or obstacles that your message needs to address from the Perceived Barriers insight, and in the Decision Criteria insight, you have confirmation that they indeed want to hear about certain features and capabilities.

These insights mean that among the many features, capabilities, and benefits discussed by the product managers and experts, we can readily isolate those that will engage your target buyers and interest them in learning more.

In many actual case studies, we've seen new features that were considered relatively unimportant to buyers, especially during the early stages of their buying journey. In other instances, there were features that the company had taken for granted that were, in fact, the most compelling way to engage select audiences.

We've also seen features, capabilities, and benefits that appear irrelevant to buyers that nevertheless provide huge value. Having never considered a need for such capabilities, buyers don't focus on these during their search and evaluation. This doesn't mean we won't include this information in our messaging. However, we need to initiate communication with buyers by addressing their primary concerns, and once they are engaged, we can then introduce additional educational information that positions our approach.

Your direction is simple: effective messaging emerges at the intersection of what your buyers want to hear and what you want to say. Some companies can find this sweet spot by adjusting their current messaging with the addition of Buyer Persona insights.

Many companies, however, need to entirely rethink their approach to messaging decisions. In the event that you're in the latter category, you might need to call a Messaging Strategy Workshop to ensure success.

Hold a Messaging Strategy Workshop

Calling for a Messaging Strategy Workshop follows the same triggering events that prompted the meeting described earlier – typically a launch or revised campaign that involves new marketing materials. Or it may be that you have just completed a Buyer Persona and gained an insight that suggests a midcourse correction to an existing messaging strategy.

The workshop's objective is to define and choose the content that will appear in the product, service, or solution messaging. However, because copywriting is an art form that should never be done by committee, no writing of actual copy will be done at these meetings. (Professionals will execute it later.) Here the objective is to carefully evaluate and select what we want the message to convey, without wrangling over the precise wording.

Participants at the workshop will include those who generally attend messaging strategy meetings at your company – they usually call on the knowledge of a solution expert as well as someone who knows the competitive landscape.

You will also want to include at least one person who is going to execute the messaging, write the website content, or compose the white paper. It's important that they understand how and why the messaging content was chosen.

Finally, you will need a moderator whose central role will be to represent the authentic voice of the Buyer Persona. When the discussion begins to focus on the appeal and importance of a particular capability, the moderator/Buyer Persona expert is available to articulate whether it is among the buyer's concerns.

Ideally, you want no more than six participants; any more than this number makes it difficult to arrive at conclusions. Should it be necessary to include others, it's best to limit their participation as observers.

The Messaging Strategy Workshop will be done in two parts, usually on two separate days, with a pre-workshop activity assigned to each participant. You will probably need about three hours for each meeting. Here is the recommended agenda for each of the meetings:

- **Day 1:** Find the intersection between what you want to say (your capabilities) and what the buyer wants to hear (their needs, goals, and concerns). This intersection is the sweet spot because it will reveal where your buyer's expectations align with your company's capabilities.
- **Day 2:** Develop your short messaging by applying two filters to the list you created on Day 1. At the end of this meeting, you will have five to six message themes plus the content you need to develop your short positioning statement or elevator pitch.

Let's look at how you might run these meetings.

Ask for Pre-meeting Contributions

Before the meeting, the moderator should request that each participant prepare a bulleted list that describes the aspects of the solution they consider the most valuable in the eyes of the buyer. Each person should produce a list of not more than 10 points. They needn't be carefully crafted or perfectly written, and they shouldn't be created in collaboration. The objective is for each participant to list the points that they believe are important.

Potentially, if you have six participants and each submits a list of ten items, you might have as many as 60 bullet points. But as there will be some degree of overlap, it will be the moderator's responsibility to organize and consolidate these submissions into general topic areas. Since this is only a quest for content, not precise language, the wording isn't crucial. This completed list is a draft of "what we want to say" about this solution. As we work through this chapter, we'll call this the *Capabilities List*.

Next, to create a bulleted list of "What the buyer wants to hear" the moderator will copy the key Buying Insight Headlines from the Buyer Persona – focusing on the Priority Initiatives, Success Factors, Perceived Barriers, and Decision Criteria insights. (The moderator need not reference the Buyer's Journey insights as these are unlikely to impact marketing messaging.)

To make it easy to refer to these headlines, we'll call this list your *Buyer's Expectations*.

Each of the participants will need to have both of these lists – the Capabilities List and Buyer's Expectations – in addition to the full Buyer Persona to reference during the meeting.

Develop a Complete List of Capabilities That Matter

Start the first meeting by asking the participants to look at the bulleted list of Buyer's Expectations to see if it contains anything that your solution can't deliver. If you don't have any way to address one of your buyer's needs, that point will not be featured in your messaging. You will want to use this insight for product management, but you should eliminate it from the working list for this meeting.

Next, taking the two lists and working with them side-by-side, go through the Buyer's Expectations one at a time, referencing the Capabilities List to find statements that describe or prove your company's ability to address that need.

Whenever a bullet point on the list of Buyer's Expectations comes up for discussion, the moderator should ensure that the team fully understands the need by reading the verbatim quotations from the Buyer Persona. The moderator should use the voice of the buyer to encourage the participants to fully consider the buyer's mindset and the details of their expectations. This focus on the specific, detailed insights discovered during the buyer interviews is the team's first step toward eliminating conventional, generic, and jargon-laden messages.

For instance, consider a marketing team that's aware that buyers are reluctant to invest in solutions that might become obsolete in a few years, a Perceived Barriers insight. Wanting to counter that concern, the participants first suggested this bullet point on their Capabilities List: "We have the flexibility to design a solution that meets your needs now and in the future."

The moderator, speaking for the buyer, reminds the team that merely telling buyers that the company has addressed this concern is insufficient. Buyers are completing a significant portion of the decision process using information found online, and their CPA means that they aren't going to read anything that isn't helpful. The moderator insists that the team needs bullet points that address the buyer's specific expectations related to "flexible designs."

To enable a meaningful discussion, the team turns back to the Buyer Persona to see if flexibility was among the buyer's Decision Criteria. If it's there, quotations from the buyer interview will explain that flexibility is about adapting to evolving industry standards and a range of technology platforms. If flexibility is not included, the team can learn about the attributes that the Buyer Persona uses to gauge the long-term viability of their suppliers.

The Moderator Is a Proxy for the Buyer

Companies are often surprised that it takes a full three hours (and sometimes longer) to find the intersection between their Capabilities List and the list of Buyer's Expectations. This process will get easier as the participants become accustomed to working with Buyer Personas, but the first time through this process is difficult for most marketers. It usually takes time for marketers to think about how they can provide clear and convincing evidence that they can meet their buyer's specific expectations.

The meeting moderator will likely need to interrupt the automatic thinking that usually results in stale, timeworn summary messages about the awesome benefits delivered by the solution under discussion. The moderator will need to point out that the buyer knows about these benefits (referencing the Success Factors insight) and that the meeting needs to focus on persuading the buyer that the company can deliver the capabilities that produce these results.

As your team works through the Capabilities List, remind them that they need not worry about the number of bullet points or expend energy trying to make them pithy and concise. The job for this team is to fully articulate any capabilities that the buyer will find relevant and helpful.

This discussion only works if the moderator can actively field questions, provide answers, or interject comments that speak in the voice of the Buyer Persona. Some will even speak as a proxy for the buyer, pressing participants to expand on their messaging by asking questions like, "Can you be more specific so that your message directly addresses my concerns? Otherwise, I'm going to look elsewhere." If a messaging suggestion is too general or doesn't sound convincing to the Buyer Persona, the moderator should counter, "That's not persuasive to me. I don't believe you."

Members of the marketing team can then respond to the moderator/ Buyer Persona with questions such as, "We want our copy to emphasize that our solution is relatively easy to use, but I get the impression you want to hear much more than that. What exactly do you need to hear from us that will convince you of that fact?"

When the messaging is refined to include the details the buyer is looking for, the moderator should reinforce the process in the buyer's voice by interjecting, "Wow! This is great. This is precisely what I am looking for."

As a final part of this first step, look at your pre-meeting Capabilities List to see if everything that seemed important to the participants has been matched to one of your Buyer's Expectations. If anything essential remains on that list, you may want to review your results to see if there is a place where that capability applies. If that isn't possible, and you have an "orphan" capability from the first day's session, you can either leave it out or consider using it in "longer-form" marketing activities (white papers, blogs, recurring messaging, etc.).

At the end of the first day's meeting, you may have one, two, or perhaps three compelling bullet points that directly address each of your Buyer's Expectations – capabilities that tell the buyer that your approach to solving their problem is an ideal match for their needs.

Apply Two Filters to Identify Message Themes and Proof Points

There will be many times when you have only a few seconds or a minute to capture your Buyer Persona's attention and persuade them to take the next step to consider you. This is one of the most challenging steps in messaging, because either you will have to choose which of the salient points to communicate or you will have to create a summary that conveys several points at once. Most marketers choose the summary approach for short messaging because no one knows which of the statements will have the desired effect. Alas, this shotgun approach tends to produce messaging that buyers describe as generic and irrelevant, such as, "We are the market-leading supplier of flexible, scalable, compatible, enterprise-wide [insert widget category here]." Of course this is all gobbledygook, but we confess, we've agreed to the use of these exact words in many messages. After several hours of sitting in a room trying to make up a message guided only by the opinions of the people in that room, we'll agree to anything. Just let me outta there!

Now that you have listened to buyers relate their stories detailing how they make their choices, you have insight into the practical and emotional aspects of your buyer's decision. You can avoid writing summaries for short-form messaging and choose the specific points that will have the most impact on the buyer's decision. Imagine the buyer's reaction when, unlike your competitors, your message communicates your ability to address one of their most cherished expectations.

We recommend that you apply two filters to the first day's Capabilities List to help you decide which of these points achieves this goal. For the first filter, you will evaluate each statement based on your competitors' ability to make that statement. The second filter requires your team to rank the capabilities based on their relative importance to your buyers.

Evaluate Your Capabilities vs. the Competition's

Working with each of the bullet points on the Capabilities List you developed during the first day of your Messaging Strategy Workshop, the participants will work together to assign one of the following numerical values to each statement:

- **1-Impossible:** Your competitors cannot claim this capability. (Be careful, this is rare.)
- **2-Difficult:** Your competitors can make this claim, but if you have a chance to tell your full story, you can clearly demonstrate your superiority.
- **3-Easy:** Your competitors can readily match this capability.

Naturally, these ratings will require some intelligence about the competition and are likely to vary for each competitor. Don't worry too much about that part of the discussion because our objective isn't a precise measurement. We are only interested in an indicator about the relative strength and weakness of the claim.

An important side effect of assigning these Competitive Ratings is that it encourages the team to adjust the content of their first-day meeting's Capabilities List statements. When people see that their generic statements result in too many Competitive Ratings of 3, they are highly motivated to revise the statement to say something more compelling and specific.

Using the sort feature on your spreadsheet, you can easily see the capability statements with the highest Competitive Rating (1) at the top, and the weakest (3) at the bottom of your list.

Assess the Relative Value of Your Capabilities to Buyers

Although the step you just completed reveals your competitive advantages in terms of their singularity, it doesn't tell you which of your capabilities is most important to your buyers. We want to consider competitive advantages as one aspect of choosing your messaging, while avoiding those unfortunate situations where the company emphasizes a unique aspect of their solution that has little or no effect on the buyer's decision.

We eliminated the risk that you will say anything that is completely irrelevant to your buyer by working from a list of Buyer's Expectations at the inception of this process. If you did survey research after developing your Buyer Persona (see Chapter 9), you will have even more guidance in terms of which Buyer's Expectations are the most influential in their buying decision. But because this step will result in messages used to initially engage the buyer, in this final step you want to identify the capabilities that most effectively address your buyer's urgent or compelling expectations.

To complete this assessment, the meeting participants need to rate the capabilities based on their relative ability to affect your buyer's decision. Doing so usually requires the participants to make a judgment call. This is accomplished by reviewing verbatim quotations in the Buyer

Persona and finding statements that evoke vivid or emotional reactions. Then with the buyer in mind, evaluate each capability to determine how well it communicates value to the persona.

Working as a team, the workshop participants rate each capability either A, B, or C. An A rating designates a capability included in messaging that the buyer will find of highest value, while B and C ratings apply to those that are likely to have a relatively lower impact.

The moderator's role is to help the participants evaluate each capability statement from two perspectives: "How much urgency does the buyer assign to this expectation?" and "How well does your statement communicate your ability to deliver what your buyer expects?"

Once you have assigned these rankings, sort your list a final time. At the top of the list, you will see those capabilities that communicate the most value to your buyers; those that have lesser value will appear in the middle, and those with the least value will fall to the bottom.

If you are lucky, you will see that a few of the capabilities at the top of your list also have a high Competitive Rating. But don't be surprised if that doesn't happen. In Figure 10.1 you can see that the statements with the most value to buyers earned a Competitive Rating of 2. Competitors can make these same statements, but when marketers or salespeople have a chance to present a long form of their message, they can prove their approach is superior.

We've also seen instances where a message that rated highest on the list of value to buyers earned only a Competitive Rating of 3. In one memorable case, a company that will remain unnamed here shipped a solution that had a number of flaws. As one of the largest suppliers in this category, this problem was highly visible to the company's prospective customers. When they initiated their Messaging Strategy Workshop they had resolved the problem and added new, differentiated capabilities that they fully expected to feature in their upcoming launch. However, by working through this process they realized their folly. The new capability barely registered as a buyer expectation. Instead, at the top of the list of value to buyers was concern about the emotional fallout that came as a consequence of the flawed release. This had been discovered during buyer interviews and appeared in the Buyer Persona as a Perceived

Source of Expectation	High-Value Capabilities	Competitive Rating	Buyer Value Rating
Priority Initiatives	Provider X's next generation 3T MRI scanners use a deep-learning image reconstruction model that prevents artifacts from being introduced into your images. This results in MRI images so clear that you can be sure that your diagnoses are detailed and accurate.	1	A
Success Factors	Created from a database of hundreds of thousands images, IMAGEx automatically detects patient anatomy and prescribes MRI slices for routine and more challenging imaging. These automated workflows create efficiencies and reproduce steps to get patients in and out of scans faster and with more imaging accuracy.	2	A
Success Factors and Decision Criteria	Provider X offers a 70 cm bore that ensures that all your patients will fit into our machines quickly and comfortably. Our innovative FLEX coil design, ambient noise, mood lighting, and video options provide a level of patient comfort and care that is unmatched in the industry.	3	A
Perceived Barriers and Decision Criteria	Over the past 30 years, nobody has invested more or earned more patents in imaging technologies and processes than Provider X. Our first-of-its-kind Imaging Research Center brings together leading minds in medicine, radiology, and imaging technology to stay at the forefront of the industry.	2	A
Decision Criteria	Led by our staff of experts, Provider X offers both online and in-person training options to ensure your team hits the ground running once your MRI machine is installed. With training facilities across the globe, Provider X conducts both on-site and classroom training based on your preferences. Our online training portal offers the most up-to-date user manuals accompanied by video tutorials and answers to frequently asked questions (FAQs).	2	A

Figure 10.1 Example of messaging strategy final ranking.

Barriers insight. The product team that had worked so hard on the new features resisted the creation of messaging that didn't emphasize their contribution. The senior executives and salespeople, however, applauded the marketing team's decision to speak directly to what mattered most to their buyers.

Bring in the Copywriters and Creative Teams

As a result of these meetings, you have a collection of capability statements that convey the information your buyers want to hear. You've sorted the list to ensure that you put the greatest emphasis on the capabilities that are most likely to persuade buyers, based on a combination of their Competitive Ratings as well as their relative value in the eyes of the buyer.

Now it's time to write the final copy. If you have the resources to employ a creative team or external resource, give them your Buyer Persona and the final spreadsheet you built during your Messaging Strategy Workshop. Be prepared to explain what you learned and how you made your decisions. If you chose well this won't take long, and soon their heads will nod in agreement as they realize you've already done a lot of hard work for them. They should understand how your insights and strategy will help them to be truly effective.

If you are writing your own copy, we won't attempt to teach you how to do it in these pages. We refer instead to others who have great advice on this topic.

However, we will ask you to ensure that whoever writes the final version of your message retains the specificity that you worked so hard to identify. Don't allow summaries, superlatives, and other forms of drivel to cloud your ability to speak directly and clearly. You and your team have invested time and effort interviewing buyers and carefully analyzing their responses to obtain Buying Insights. You have defined the intersection between what you have to say and what your buyers want to hear. Unless you have a huge budget to spend on branding a message, such as Nike's "Just Do It," your message needs to speak plainly and simply. It should help buyers like those in your Buyer Persona discover that your approach is an ideal fit for their needs. Stay firmly focused on that goal and you'll make good decisions.

> We streamlined our messaging to the most important touch points, to the kind of education buyers actually want. Now we can say to our colleagues, "These are the messages we need to say and why."
>
> —*Marketing Director*

Summary

In this chapter, we covered the following points:

- Catching a buyer's attention amid the streaming torment of information coming at them is one of the greatest challenges of contemporary marketing.
- Your messaging decisions must take into account your company's goals to communicate the value of its solutions as well as your buyer's attitudes, needs, and concerns.
- To develop effective messaging, call for a Messaging Strategy Workshop to determine the intersection of what you want to say and what your buyers want to know. This meeting will take place over two days with a pre-meeting activity assigned to each workshop participant.
- Messaging Strategy Workshop – Pre-meeting Activity:
  - Participants will prepare a bulleted list that describes up to ten aspects of your solution they consider the most valuable to your buyers. A moderator will organize and consolidate the submissions into general topic areas called your Capabilities List.
  - The moderator will also consolidate the insight headlines from the Buyer Persona – focusing on Priority Initiatives, Success Factors, Perceived Barriers, and Decision Criteria insights. This is your list of Buyer's Expectations.

- Message Strategy Workshop – Day 1:
  - Meeting participants will identify statements from the Capabilities List that describe or prove your company's ability to meet each of the Buyer's Expectations.
  - At the end of the meeting, you may have one, two, or perhaps three compelling bullet points that directly address each of your Buyer's Expectations.
- Message Strategy Workshop – Day 2:
  - Assign a Competitive Rating to each capability statement from 1 (competitors cannot easily claim this capability) to 3 (competitors can readily match this capability).
  - Assign a Buyer Value Rating to each capability statement from A to C, where A designates a capability that buyers will value the highest and C the lowest.
  - Sort this exercise by the Buyer Value Ratings and prioritize messaging based on the A ratings. Use Competitive Ratings to guide decisions on which capabilities to use in your messaging.
- Assign a copywriter and your creative team to draft the final messaging. Review it to ensure it's plain, simple, and directly speaks to how your capabilities address an important buyer expectation.

11

Adjust Strategies to Deliver the Knowledge and Experience Buyers Want

When figuring out your messaging strategy and what to say to buyers, you will want to look across your buyer's Priority Initiatives, Success Factors, Perceived Barriers, and Decision Criteria. These are your buyer's most important requirements and should have a prominent place in your messaging, particularly when you have unique capabilities to address them.

The opportunities to leverage Buyer Persona insights go beyond messaging, however. Because the 5 Rings of Buying Insight reveal everything your buyers need to know and experience to have confidence buying from you, you should leverage each insight in other important ways. Since we can't cover all the creative ways in which we've seen organizations use these insights, we'll focus this chapter on the major ideas or ways of thinking you can use to develop your own strategies.

It's worth noting that a single thread cuts across all of them. That is the fundamental buying truth we covered in Chapter 1: *the organization that does the best job of making a buyer feel CONFIDENT and SECURE in their buying decision usually wins the business.* Without much difficulty, you should readily see how everything we'll discuss here contributes to that overall objective. It's also a filter you can use to develop your own strategies and how you decide to leverage Buyer Persona insights to influence buyers.

Another lens to look through is how we can use the 5 Rings of Buying Insight to help sales overcome *customer inaction*, one of their biggest impediments to closing more deals that we discussed in Chapter 2. Whether buyers are anxious that something could go wrong if they make a change (*inability to make a decision*) or they don't see enough value versus what they're currently doing (*preference for the status quo*), helping sales overcome the reservations that interested buyers have during the latter stages of the sales cycle will have a profound impact on revenue and the value of marketing.

Empathize with Buyers Through Priority Initiatives

Have you ever met someone and had an instant connection with them? Think of a time where you met someone you didn't know and in a relatively short period of time you felt like you both understood each other. You were "speaking the same language." You were "on the same page." You may have even thought to yourself, "I really like this person, maybe we can become friends." This initial interaction, even if brief, created a connection where trust and a mutually beneficial relationship could grow.

It's safe to say that we've all had these types of connections in our lives – ideally many times if we're lucky! Without personally being privy to encounters you have had like this, we're willing to wager the other person involved attentively listened to your perspective (regardless of the topic), understood what you were saying, and was able to appreciate it.

As a result, you felt heard, understood, and respected. Assuming you did the same for them, the feeling was likely mutual.

Within your Buyer Persona, Priority Initiatives are your pathway to developing an initial connection with prospective buyers just like this. Priority Initiatives are the circumstances and pain points that trigger a buyer to look for a solution like yours. The vast majority of buyers didn't wake up one day and have these challenges. They have had them for a while and are looking for providers that can quickly and clearly signal to them: "Yes, we understand your situation, and we can help." And because you talked to buyers to develop your Buyer Persona, you know what their Priority Initiatives are with the clarity, depth, and nuance that will be tough for your competitors to match.

There's a few ways to do this in your marketing:

- Acknowledge your buyer's Priority Initiatives early on in their buying journey – whether it be through a website, lead campaigns, thought leadership, events, sales, or any other mechanism where you are likely to first encounter prospective buyers. Recognizing and empathizing with your buyer's Priority Initiatives creates the initial connection that sparks interest in what you have to offer. It's also a stepping-stone to the role of a trusted advisor, where you can confidently guide buyers through their buying journey as they evaluate their options and make a decision.
- Develop messaging and longer-form communications (white papers, blogs, recurring messaging) that demonstrate how your organization's unique capabilities and solution features address a buyer's Priority Initiatives.
- Build case studies and customer references that demonstrate how your capabilities and solution are the antidote to your buyer's Priority Initiatives by alleviating the pain they are in.

Build Buyer Trust and Confidence Through Success Factors

If you were around in the mid-1980s, you might remember an ad campaign for the Wendy's fast-food chain where an elderly woman received a hamburger from another quick-serve restaurant and famously says "Where's the beef?" Picture an oversized bun and a hamburger the size of a silver dollar and you get the gist. In one of the funnier television spots for the Wendy's campaign, the woman and her two friends examine a burger like this at the checkout counter of one of these other chains where a sign on the back wall reads: "Home of the Big Bun." In a light and satirical way, the "Where's the beef?" campaign became a huge success because Wendy's was cleverly able to point out something fundamental to any buying decision (even something as simple as a burger) – buyers want to receive something they value for the money they're spending.

Within your Buyer Persona, Success Factors are the most important outcomes that buyers want as a result of their investment in your solution – they are the proverbial "beef." Success Factors are often the opposite side of the Priority Initiatives coin. While Priority Initiatives highlight the pain points that have become too difficult to bear, Success Factors are the tangible outcomes that buyers expect to obtain from their investment. This is what they want as a result of doing business with you (no pressure!).

There are several ways to use Success Factors to your advantage in marketing:

- Similar to Priority Initiatives, focus interactions and messaging on Success Factors early on in the buying journey so buyers quickly see that you understand the outcomes that they seek.
- Develop thought leadership on the benefits of buying your solution and how specific features can enable a buyer to achieve the outcomes they care about most. Make the linkage from features to Success Factors as clear and direct as you can so buyers don't have to figure out the connection themselves.
- Build case studies and customer references directly tied to Success Factors. Recall that one of the greatest impediments to sales is a buyer's *inability to make a decision* because they're anxious something could go wrong. To help sales overcome these objections, develop case studies that demonstrate how other customers have

achieved the same outcomes the buyer is looking for. Include details about how your capabilities and solution features overcame the obstacles that buyers are concerned about most, so they have confidence that the pathway to success is achievable.

■ Where possible, highlight specific and measurable performance improvements that other customers have achieved across each of the Success Factors. This will help sales overcome *preference for the status quo*, where buyers don't perceive enough value to make the investment versus sticking with what they're currently doing.

■ Develop or review your business case template to make sure it includes your Buyer Persona's Success Factors.

At a recent trade when visitors crossed the aisle to come to our booth, they asked what made us different. The persona work had made it easy for us to communicate differentiation. In fact, it was the most successful trade show we've ever done!

—*Senior Vice President, Marketing*

Differentiate Through Perceived Barriers

Perceived Barriers reveal everything that prevents buyers from considering your solution and why some may think your competitors have a better approach. These are all the things that either eliminated a provider from consideration or winnowed them out at some point in the evaluation process. Although this sounds doom and gloom, Perceived Barriers actually provide you with the best opportunity to differentiate yourself. Why? Because, if you have the capabilities to confidently address a Perceived Barrier, you can be certain that some providers do not.

Lean in to Perceived Barriers in the following ways to distinguish yourself:

■ Develop marketing messages around any Perceived Barriers that your organization and solution can address. Provide as much detail and substantiation as you can. By offering specifics you'll provide buyers with concrete evidence that builds their confidence in buying from you. In contrast, if you're vague or ambiguous, that will only heighten a buyer's suspicions that you cannot really deliver.

For example, magnetic resonance imaging (MRI) machine buyers expressed concerns about working with a manufacturer that doesn't have technical support resources in close proximity to their hospital. If an MRI manufacturer had a deeper and geographically broader bench of technical support resources than other providers, it's something they would want to highlight in their messaging.

- Address Perceived Barriers in your case studies and client references to the extent of what's possible. It's one thing for you to claim it, it's another thing for one of your clients to substantiate that claim with their own experience.
- Develop Frequently Asked Questions (FAQs) for Perceived Barriers. Since these buyer concerns are top-of-mind and eliminate providers from contention, address as many as you can so buyers can readily see that you have the capabilities to ease their fears. Use these in your sales playbooks too if you have them.
- Develop additional sales enablement assets that your salesforce can use to address Perceived Barriers. This will demonstrate to buyers that your sellers are aware of their concerns, are interested in alleviating them, and have the capabilities to do so.

When thinking about the different ways to use Perceived Barriers, remember that buyers are uneasy about this high-consideration buying decision. They either haven't made it before or haven't made it frequently. By proactively addressing their concerns, you're giving them the assurances they crave, building their confidence that this investment will work out, and showing them that your organization is best suited to deliver the outcomes they seek.

Answer Important Buyer Questions Through Decision Criteria

Decision Criteria are the nitty-gritty attributes of your product, service, or solution that buyers evaluate as they compare their options. In the Buyer Persona we communicate these Buying Insights in the form of a question because buyers will ask you about them either directly or indirectly as they get deeper into their buying journey and become more educated about the different options available to them. Relative to Priority Initiatives, Success Factors, and Perceived Barriers, you will typically see more Decision Criteria because the number and specificity of buyer questions increase as they winnow down their choices and take a harder look at the alternatives they're considering.

Because of this, we recommend examining Decision Criteria in two ways. The first way is to *look for a smaller set of themes across the Decision Criteria* to simplify your understanding of them and identify broader categories that you may be able to address in different ways. We sometimes refer to these as "the insights within the insights." As an example, here's the six broader themes we identified within the 11 MRI machine Decision Criteria (Figures 8.4 and 8.5):

- **How sharp, clear, and detailed is your imaging quality?** The strength of the machine's magnet is related to this Decision Criteria as well.
- **How quickly and easily can we complete a scan?** Speed of scan sequences and a simple and efficient user interface (UI) and workflow tie to this Decision Criteria.
- **Can we make patients more comfortable and improve their experience?** Several Decision Criteria link to this including scanning speed, bore size, coil options, and value-add features that improve the patient's experience in the machine.
- **Will you get us up and running quickly and provide the ongoing support we need?** Speed and reliability of implementation, quality of training, and local after-sale support are all important elements of this broader theme.

- **Will you continue to innovate and keep us at or ahead of the industry?** When buyers want to understand your product roadmap, this is the essence of why they care.
- **What is the total cost of ownership (TCO) and can we generate a positive return on investment (ROI)?** Buyers want to make sure there are no surprises when it comes to TCO so that they can build a credible business case to which the hospital will buy in.

The second way to use Decision Criteria is to *look at them one-by-one* because each reveals the specific attributes of your solution that buyers will evaluate closely. For example, the quality of coil options is part of the broader theme of making patients more comfortable, but it is also important to know that buyers will be investigating coils very specifically too.

Whether using the broader Decision Criteria themes or each of them individually, here's a few ways to leverage these buyer requirements in your marketing efforts:

- Provide as much detail and substantiation as you can about how you will address each Decision Criteria through your value propositions, messages, and longer-form marketing mechanisms (blogs, white papers, recurring messages, etc.). Details build a buyer's trust; generalizations and ambiguity erode the hard work you have completed to this point.
- Show side-by-side comparisons of your capabilities and features across each Decision Criteria compared to the other alternatives that buyers may be considering. At this point, buyers are trying to sort through and make sense of all the information that is coming at them as they evaluate their options. Make it easy on them and cast a light on what differentiates you best.

  For example, in the case of the MRI machine, if a manufacturer has data showing it takes less time to conduct certain types of scan sequences using its machine compared to machines from other providers, they should make those comparisons evident to buyers. If you don't think these differences matter, think again. As one MRI machine buyer told us:

- *"We looked at the time for the sequences – how long it takes for each individual one. For example, for a brain MRI, Company D takes 12 minutes versus Company B who takes 14 minutes. Those small nuances and their algorithms are important. They change the timing, and it allows for different numbers of procedures to be done in a day, which plays a large role in our overall workflow."*

- Develop FAQs for each Decision Criteria. Much like Perceived Barriers, buyers will appreciate that you are clearly and directly answering the most important questions that they have. Use these in your sales playbooks too if you have them.

- Show how each Decision Criteria, and your ability to address them, will enable buyers to achieve their Priority Initiatives and Success Factors. Using the MRI machine example, an MRI machine manufacturer could link bore size, coil options, and value-add features (Decision Criteria) to improving a patient's scan experience (Success Factors). Making this linkage strengthens your value proposition and makes it easier for buyers to see how specific features of your solution lead to the outcomes they care about most.

- Incorporate answers to Decision Criteria in sales pitches and solution demos so buyers have confidence that you can address all their important questions.

- If your organization uses a product-led growth (PLG) approach, leverage Decision Criteria insights to develop strategies that demonstrate important features of your solution through trials and other forms of buyer interaction with your product.

The persona insights told us what was key to say – and not to say. These insights contributed to a new tagline – "We Stop Cloud-Native Attacks" – and to a deeper awareness of customer journey stages. It helped us build specific marketing elements for different stages: what to say to whom, when.

—*Chief Marketing Officer*

Design Marketing Activities to Enable Your Buyer's Journey

When you think about the best way to engage buyers, you are likely to be confronted by a bewildering variety of options. In his book *Youtility*, digital marketing strategist and best-selling author Jay Baer suggests some simple but surprising guidance to anyone facing this quandary: "Your marketing should be so useful that people would gladly pay for it."

We are not suggesting that your buyers should offer their credit card information in exchange for your white paper or webinar. Rather that this value is one of the standards you should apply to every marketing decision. Focus on designing your lead generation campaign to make it more useful to your buyers.

Should you offer an extremely valuable asset after you ask your buyers to "pay" with their name and e-mail address? Or should you forego the registration until you have given your buyers something useful for free? Would you describe yourself as the market-leading provider of flexible, scalable, compatible, easy-to-use widgets if you wanted to help your buyers evaluate your solution's applicability for their needs?

The perfect time to be useful begins when your buyer decides to prioritize an investment in a solution much like the one you are offering. At this moment, you don't have to be pushy or particularly clever to get their attention. Now your buyer is looking for the information to help them to assess your ability to address their requirements.

If you have done your buyer interviews, you know that this Buyer Persona has a specific goal – your Priority Initiatives insight – and is doing considerable work to understand who is best qualified to deliver on expectations – Success Factors, Perceived Barriers, and Decision Criteria insights. Even if your solution is more expensive, you can earn your buyer's trust by delivering the answers they want to hear through the resources they trust – revealed in your Buyer's Journey insight. One of the most important uses of your Buyer Persona is to help you deliver the useful marketing content that makes this assessment easy for your buyers.

Although you want to draw interest in your solution's category, let's establish that your most urgent goal is to be useful to people at the moment they are researching and asking questions about solutions like the one you offer. Buyers at this stage of their journey will make their decision far sooner than those who aren't yet looking. Accordingly, this comprises the shortest pathway from insights to leads and revenue. If that isn't motivation enough, consider the implications if you mount a successful effort to bring people into the top of your sales funnel and then disappoint them once they begin to engage with you.

When you understand your Buyer Persona and focus on creating useful information, you create the trust that inspires them to initiate a relationship with you. As Jay Baer says, "There are two ways for companies to succeed in this era: be amazing or be useful. The latter is much more reliable and viable."

Prioritize Assets That Align with the Buyer's Journey

We've seen solution marketers who build and maintain upwards of 200 assets for each of their solutions. The Buyer's Journey is extremely valuable in its capability to help the marketing team prioritize their activities and deliverables, and thus reduce that large number of assets dramatically.

In our MRI machine Buyer Persona, it is easy to see how the Buyer's Journey will help a manufacturer's marketing team focus on the assets that will have the most impact on a prospective buyer's decision. For example:

- Noting that buyers learn about these solutions through online research and industry resources, these marketers are giving priority to their online presence and healthcare-focused journals, white papers, and conferences.
- The Buying Insights indicate that buyers are heavily influenced by peer input during the research phase, so the team will closely monitor social media, user forums, and customer service records for early warning of any downturn in customer satisfaction or brand reputation.
- Reflecting on the buyers' visits to vendor websites and their Success Factors, Perceived Barriers, and Decision Criteria, the

manufacturer will prominently feature analyst reports, customer references, and videos about reducing scan times, producing higher-quality images, and improving the patient experience.

- To enable the salespeople to excel during the initial vendor meetings, the team will build a sales playbook that communicates their Buying Insights and how to confidently address each of the Perceived Barriers concerns and Decision Criteria requirements.
- The team will also maintain and cultivate relationships with their current customers in key locations around the country that enable prospective buyers to conduct site visits quickly and easily. To prepare customers for the buyer visits, they will develop a checklist with recommendations about the scanning sequences and product's features that buyers are likely to be the most interested in and how to best show them.
- They will slightly rewrite their case studies to ensure that the most compelling aspects of their message are communicated in the first few paragraphs.
- And finally, the team will review their business-case template to make sure it includes Priority Initiatives and Success Factors that buyers identify as important.

Rather than developing a standard set of marketing tools for every solution, the Buyer's Journey gave these marketers the confidence to prioritize assets that are the most helpful for MRI machine buyers and salespeople. This will increase the ROI of their efforts and substantially reduce their workload.

Changing the Conversation with Salespeople

Ask your most successful salespeople to describe their winning strategy, and they will undoubtedly talk about the trusted relationships they build with their customers. Sure, they need to understand your products, the competitive landscape, and how to deliver a compelling presentation. And yes, they want good leads and sales tools. But their core priority is to create strong customer partnerships. That's how they increase win rates and gain momentum in their territory.

With this simple explanation of the sales persona, think about your last meeting with that team. Did you talk about your upcoming promotional event, how many leads you hope to deliver, or maybe that product launch that's coming in the next few months? Were the salespeople listening to you, or were they preoccupied with their smartphones?

Imagine the change in their response if you started your next meeting by talking about the Buying Insights you've discovered through recent interviews. After all, in the course of your interviews you will have learned a great deal of information about the people they need to engage and will have details about what goes on behind the scenes that your buyers have never revealed to their salesperson.

Now you can tell your salespeople the good news: Our research confirms that these types of buyers want to meet with you, *and* not only do we know the reasons why, we also know what they hope to hear from you as well. We know which types of buyers are in the buying center, what they object to, and what they are going to love.

This will get their attention. We promise. *Now* your reps are ready to hear about the marketing activities and sales tools you've created to help these buyers see the value of your approach.

Share Insights, Not Buyer Personas

One caveat, however. As with all communications, consider your audience. You want to provide information to salespeople in a format that they trust, will be receptive to, and that they can use. The Buyer Persona typically satisfies none of these criteria.

Since salespeople are correctly trained to view every customer as unique, they tend to be suspicious that it's possible to create an example buyer. Show up at a meeting with your Buyer Persona and the first slide they'll see is your Buyer Profile. Surprised by this unexpected contribution from marketing, they are likely to focus on one demographic detail and summarily discount all of the valuable findings you plan to deliver in the upcoming Buying Insight slides. They might say:

> Wait, I had lunch with that guy yesterday. He's got that job, but he doesn't report to the CEO [chief executive officer]. He reports to the CTO [chief technology officer]. What else is wrong here?

You might eventually be able to explain the methodology in this book, but we urge you to avoid this potential problem altogether and deliver your Buyer Persona insights in a format that's the most useful and easiest to digest.

We advise you to leave your Buyer Profile in the marketing department and help your salespeople understand your Buying Insights, which your salespeople will readily recognize as the intelligence that will help them anticipate their buyers' needs, concerns, and priorities. As you stand at the front of the room, you can say "We've been interviewing people who have recently evaluated MRI machines, including people who chose us and those who bought from the 'big time' competitor. Here's what we learned."

Deliver Buying Insights Through Sales Playbooks

One of the most helpful ways to communicate Buying Insights to salespeople is by integrating them into existing sales tools such as sales playbook or training courses. Salespeople don't need another resource to consult; instead, they should be able to access your Buyer Persona intelligence in a format they have come to rely upon and access regularly.

Because sales playbooks are typically organized around buying decisions or solutions, it should be relatively easy to see how you can update them to include the insights you collected through your interviews. For example, in the section defining all of the people involved in the buying decision: job titles, responsibilities, and experience, you may add any relevant information from your Buyer Profile. You may have to adjust the template somewhat but see if you can include information about the dynamics between these influencers, especially the way that each of these buyers impacts the buying decision – a Buyer's Journey insight.

Another section of the report should focus on the key points that a salesperson should communicate. This is the place to incorporate the work that you did in Chapter 10, where you identified the intersection between what your buyers want to hear and your strongest capabilities.

As most playbooks include a section on competitors, be sure to include your Perceived Barriers insights along with the message points that will help your salesperson overcome those objections and debunk the myths. You may also find some of these points in the Decision

Criteria insights, especially if your buyers have expectations where there is a perceived gap or your approach is unexpected.

Summary

In this chapter, we covered the following points:

- Acknowledge Priority Initiatives early on in your Buyer's Journey to establish an initial connection with them. Develop messaging and longer-form communications to demonstrate how your unique capabilities can help alleviate the challenges they face.
- Focus on capabilities and solution features that enable buyers to achieve their Success Factors. Develop (or adjust) case studies and customer references so they demonstrate how other customers have achieved the outcomes that buyers care about most.
- Use Perceived Barriers to differentiate. Develop marketing messages, case studies, FAQs, and sales enablement assets that demonstrate how your capabilities can alleviate a buyer's fears and concerns.
- Use Decision Criteria to anticipate and guide how you answer the questions that buyers use to evaluate their options. Draw comparisons to competitors where you have distinct advantages. Link solution features to desired outcomes (Priority Initiatives and Success Factors) to help buyers see a direct pathway to success.
- Develop strategies and prioritize marketing assets to enable your Buyer's Journey. Focus marketing on those things that help buyers make an educated and confident buying decision; eliminate or deprioritize those that don't.
- Share Buying Insights, not Buyer Personas with sales. Doing so will ensure they pay attention and use the findings to their advantage. Delivering these insights through sales playbooks can be very effective since it's a format many are used to and rely on already.

12

Start Small, with an Eye to the Future

Knowledge is power.

These three words appear in quotations that have been cited and repeated countless times. An Internet search attributes this phrase to a wide variety of familiar names ranging from Sir Francis Bacon and Kofi Anan to Tom Clancy and Mary J. Blige.

Perhaps a cliché, and yet, as with most clichés, within it resides the truth.

It's a theme that appears in numerous episodes of the original *Star Trek* series, in stories about people who become powerful after acquiring new knowledge. The inhabitants of a troubled planet who followed the instructions of an idol or a disembodied brain learn that their leadership is merely an illusion, a machine, or a supremely fallible mortal. Once the truth is revealed to the citizens of the planet, our heroes, Captain Kirk and his crew, warped away on the *Enterprise,* leaving the inhabitants to take control of their lives.

We can't promise that the knowledge and insights that you will gain by interviewing your buyers will make you a hero, but we do know that you will have the power to quickly affect dramatic change in your company and take more control over the strategies we've discussed.

201

The logic is inescapable. Your buyer interviews will give you insight into the factors that influence buyers' decisions. With this clearly defined information, you can become a trusted authoritative resource within your company: the one person to consult for guidance on messaging and activities intended to convince buyers to choose your organization's solution. As the source of Buying Insight, you will possess the knowledge your sales people need to align the strategies intended to win your buyer's business.

You may choose to stop there. But before we end, we want to reveal just a bit more about potential ways to leverage Buyer Personas.

Where to Begin Your Buyer Persona Initiative

Over the years we've presented the concepts in this book to experienced marketers at countless seminars and workshops. When they realize they can use Buyer Personas to focus their strategies and achieve their goals, the energy and sense of excitement in the room is almost palpable.

Yet we'll never forget the marketer who approached us at the end of the session: "Wow! This is the most amazing idea I've ever heard. It's so logical. And it has the power to change my life."

And then he changed the tone of his voice. "The only problem is that you are assuming our management is logical."

Persuading key stakeholders – either the decision-makers within your organization or a client of your marketing agency – can be difficult. Stakeholders who express reluctance to engage in Buyer Persona research sometimes worry that if they go down this path they may need to build personas for every product in their company.

Contrasting with this resistance, there are the extremely excited visionaries who begin imagining all the potential possibilities. Marketers at large companies tell me, "We really want to do this! I want to build personas across all of our solutions, for every decision buyers make, for every buyer we know." As excited as we are too, we strongly urge you not to undertake anything like this. Not yet anyway.

You will want to start with one well-defined project, goal, or campaign of strategic interest to your stakeholders. It should be one that everyone agrees cannot be achieved by doing business as usual. With the outcome defined as something your stakeholders acknowledge will be difficult, you will have established the grounds to test the value of your Buyer Persona initiative. And once you can point to proven results, you will have earned support for using Buyer Personas to make future decisions about the messaging and activities that engage buyers to choose you.

Choosing the right place to begin may seem a bit daunting, but the selection of a challenging goal will make it more difficult for anyone to claim after the fact that your results could have been obtained without your Buyer Persona.

For example, your organization may be entering markets that require your salespeople to call on an entirely new type of buyer. Or you may want to market a solution that combines an existing product with one that was acquired through a merger. Or perhaps your company is suddenly experiencing competitive pressure in a market where you had previously been the acknowledged leader.

If your company has been struggling with these problems, it is highly likely that the insight from this single project will be met with surprise . . . possibly astonishment. Where previously the path to success was unknown, your stakeholders will now understand the Priority Initiatives that cause buyers to take action, the Success Factors that motivate them, and the Perceived Barriers that have been thwarting your efforts. Rather than a mass or scattershot campaign, the Buyer's Journey will show them which buyers are most critical to reach, and through your Decision Criteria insights, they'll know whether your solution and company has what it takes to win this business.

You want a dramatic demonstration that shows that a small, focused Buyer Persona initiative can make a lasting impression. Only after this impression has been made dramatically and forcefully – and won over allies and convinced influential stakeholders – should you begin to build Buyer Personas for other parts of your business.

Don't be concerned about going slowly. We know of no companies that have fully integrated Buyer Personas into all of the activities detailed in the pages of this book. As of this writing, even the major corporations that are using this methodology have only focused on select marketing initiatives.

> We've engaged 8100 new security buyers this year, nearly doubling the 4400 from all of last year. These new contacts have increased security-related sales.
>
> —*Chief Marketing Officer*

How to Earn Your Stripes as a Strategic Resource

It is our vision that once stakeholders begin to trust Buyer Personas to guide their decisions, they will start thinking of marketers as the buyer experts; authorities who can be counted upon to guide the company's strategies to reach new markets, achieve difficult goals, or overcome competitive obstacles.

We've always noticed that no one questions the assumption that the finance team is best qualified to keep the books, or that engineering is most knowledgeable about building useful products. But marketing tends to be everyone's playground.

One reason for this contrasting perception of disciplines is the fact that unlike other professional roles, marketers have not been positioned as the owners of specialized, high-value competencies. Senior management entrusts the IT department with complex decisions because they have extensive knowledge of available technologies and how they can be applied to the company's business.

Once marketers are perceived as buyer experts, they should be given similar authority to affect decisions that impact buyers and customers. From acquisitions to market expansion and product extensions, the buyer's perspective is of utmost importance to the success or failure of these initiatives. There is currently a vacuum of Buying Insight inside most corporations. Marketers need to own that competency.

We have no illusions that this transformation will occur swiftly and suddenly. But small changes can make a big difference. Consider the way many marketers speak in meetings. It's common for marketers to preface their remarks with phrases such as, "I think," or "From where I sit, it seems to me that. . . ." Instead, marketers should strive to remove the first-person pronouns and channel the authority of the buyer's voice.

At any meeting where your buyers' opinion is relevant, make an effort to start your sentence with, "We've been listening to buyers and here's what they think," or "We have been interviewing buyers and they said they wanted. . . ."

As a proxy for your buyer, you should have the confidence to speak with authority and bring your buyer's voice to that decision. Making statements such as these may raise questions about how recently you have spoken to these buyers, so be prepared to back up your comments. If you are conducting your own interviews, we generally recommend that you conduct one interview a month, as this makes it easy to provide the answer everyone wants to hear.

In reality, however, it may surprise you that Buying Insights do not change as often as you think, and when they do, you will likely be aware that you need to engage in additional interviews. That's because the primary triggers for these changes are big news – a major upturn or downturn in economic conditions, the merger or divestiture initiated by a significant competitor, or a new government regulation that requires your customers to make an investment in a solution like the one your organization offers. Major advances in technology or security problems are other factors that affect Buying Insights, but once again, these will be highly obvious to you and everyone else. If any of these occur, and depending on the severity of the change, you will want to invest in another round of interviews to understand how your buyer's mindset may have shifted.

If you use a third party to conduct your buyer interviews, and if no significant changes have occurred, you might consider asking your vendor to conduct a few new interviews once every six months or year. It is highly unlikely that the changes will be substantive, but this should handle the perception that your insights are not current enough to rely upon.

Communicating Insights That Affect Other Teams

As you listen to your buyers describe their experience evaluating your existing solutions, you are likely to learn about non-marketing-related matters that are affecting your ability to win their business.

These opportunities are most likely to show up as part of your buyers' Decision Criteria or Perceived Barriers, revealing that your company is not meeting your buyer's expectations in the area of sales, service, or product functionality. It could be that your product doesn't effectively integrate with a particular network or infrastructure. Maybe it doesn't create the kind of reports that are in demand. Or perhaps your reputation for sales and implementation services is having an unfavorable impact on your buyer's decision.

We advise you to be cautious when you make any of these discoveries, especially if this is your first Buyer Persona and you are still working to gain the confidence of your internal stakeholders. Remember that your primary goal is to gain guidance for changes that will improve your marketing activities.

For example, if you hear that your buyers consistently have the same incorrect perception about your solution, avoid the impulse to complain to sales that they are failing to communicate correctly with potential buyers. Instead, your first step is to own the problem and invest in marketing activities intended to debunk the misperception. If this is one of your buyer's critical expectations, make it one of the key messages on your website or create an e-book about your approach. Reinforce the need for sales to emphasize that capability in your sales training or playbooks.

But once you've taken these steps and won your stakeholder's support for the value that Buyer Personas deliver to marketing, you may want to take your product-related findings to your development team. If there are sales-related problems, we urge you to take that finding to a senior manager in marketing and ask them to facilitate the communication to sales management. This will be a sensitive conversation and you don't want to do anything that might interfere with your ability to continue to conduct these valuable interviews.

The pipeline experienced triple digit growth after the new messaging was provided. Our sales reps really appreciate the new messaging. It makes their lives easier because we're telling them how to win!

—*Vice President, Product Marketing*

Using Buyer Personas to Guide Strategic Planning

Let's look into the future and consider marketing's new role in strategic planning once Buyer Personas have become an accepted part of your company's marketing activities and your marketing team is positioned as the company's respected buyer experts.

Whenever we talk to the technology industry, we can't address the subject of strategic planning without the name Steve Jobs being raised during the conversation. Jobs, who was legendary for his visionary foresight, was also well known for rejecting the value of market research. But one of the reasons Steve Jobs is legendary is that he was unique. He possessed an exceptional, perhaps genius-level ability to perceive market problems and needs and use this knowledge to drive the strategic direction of his company.

On occasions when people ask us about Jobs' attitude toward market research, this is our honest response: "If you've got a Steve Jobs in your company, don't listen to me a minute longer. Go sit at his feet, listen to what he has to say and do whatever he tells you. But if you're working with mere mortals in a typical company, you'll want to have a methodology that produces the insight you need to make buyer-focused decisions."

Of the countless decisions that your company makes, among the most challenging are the choices in the strategic plan. This is where your senior-level executives make commitments of resources and budget by evaluating their opportunities for growth in the coming years.

At the table are members of the C-suite offices, including the Chief Marketing Officer (CMO), who is expected, among other topics, to recommend a marketing budget that will support the company's projected revenue growth. Most often, these decisions are guided by historical patterns of investments and returns. If there is any "market data" in the room, it is likely based on analyst predictions about the growth in your core markets.

Now, the company must use this data to project its revenue and, for larger companies, decide which of several solutions will make the biggest contribution. As many companies determine the marketing budget as a percentage of revenue, you can imagine the tension in the room. The CMO wants the right budget, but no one wants to forecast a revenue number that the team cannot achieve.

We envision a future where another source will add significant intelligence to this decision. At this point you will have Buyer Personas for most of your current products plus those that will launch during the coming year. For the first time, your CMO can design and defend their marketing plans based on what buyers are saying about the resources they need and the places they expect to find them. They can justify the investment in marketing to a new audience with insight about that buying influencer's role to initiate the purchase or choose the provider. They can even defend the decision to invest far less than, or far more than, the industry average for marketing expenses as a share of revenue, because they have a clear case to invest in a strategy that will win more business.

In our vision, you will have included questions about your buyer's top priorities for the coming year, so your CMO can also guide decisions about which products need the most investment. Now, they can say, "Let's not put our bets on product A next year, because it's really product C that buyers say is their priority."

Perhaps you will have also invested in another interviewing technique that provides more visionary insight into the long-range priorities for specific buyers. In contrast to the interviews with buyers about recent decisions, these interviews focus on larger trends and conceptual issues in the marketplace. It's an advanced skill that calls for the experience of a professional interviewer, or someone who has already become comfortably adept at conducting probing inquiries. These interviews would help your CMO to identify buyer needs years in advance, with questions such as:

- How will the use of artificial intelligence (AI) change the way business is done?
- Where will the growth in computing power take us next?
- Where is the idea of driverless cars going?
- What is the next evolution in green housing?

Unlike the buyer stories featured throughout this book, these interviews require you to introduce a topic that the buyer may or may not have contemplated. It is extremely easy to bias the outcome of these interviews and as a result, collect data that is unreliable. So, with a recommendation that such exchanges are best conducted by an experienced interviewer, here, nevertheless, is the concept.

The first question should be defined around an issue or priority that your company hopes will be relevant in the coming years. For instance, your opening question might be "We've been interviewing a number of retailers about drone delivery services, and one of the things we're hearing is their concern about the drone's limited battery life. We are hearing deep concern that gas-powered engines appear to be the far more practical option. What are your thoughts about that?"

Alternatively, you might want to explore the financial considerations of this solution, asking a different question, "We've been talking to other retailers about delivery drones, and we're hearing that this is going allow them to deliver more items while cutting both their manpower and delivery time. They report they are now starting to make huge investments in this technology and are rushing to be among the first to offer this service. What are your thoughts about that?"

The model for beginning this kind of interview is, "We've been talking to other people like you and one of the things we're hearing . . ." and then you insert a trend or issue that you see developing in the market that your company wants to capitalize on, followed by a conclusion that's somewhat provocative.

The reason we want to make it provocative is that we want to elicit an emotional reaction from the buyer. Some will respond, "No way! Those batteries only last ten minutes and that isn't going to help me, except in very dense markets. I would love to use a gasoline-powered engine, but my customers aren't going to want a noisy weed-whacker flying over their heads." Or, "This is a Buck Rogers fantasy. We're not going to invest in this." Or you might get the buyer who says, "Absolutely, we agree completely. Gas-powered engines are the only way delivery drones are going to happen, and here's why. . . ."

With these reactions you can begin to get a sense of buyers' current attitudes around a solution that your company sees as a part of your long-term strategy. It's a completely different method of conducting buyer interviews, and we caution you not to start here, but in combination with the fundamental interviewing covered throughout the book, we predict a future where your CMO will have increasingly valuable input to your company's most strategic decisions.

Start Small and Make a Difference

No one we know is utilizing Buyer Personas in all of these ways. Keep these more advanced ideas filed away until you are in a position to use them.

Despite all the exciting things you may want to accomplish, we urge you to go slowly and start with one critical project. You will never have the opportunity to explore any of these possibilities unless you can establish the credibility, authority, and influence of Buyer Personas with your first project. We remind you to choose one focused yet difficult project, goal, or campaign that is acknowledged to be of strategic importance to all stakeholders – and make a big statement about the value of Buyer Personas.

Buyer Personas are an incredibly powerful tool when used correctly. We know from working with thousands of business professionals that the methodology detailed in this book can achieve all the things we've described in the first 11 chapters of this book. In this chapter we have given you a glimpse of the impressive future that you might experience as you master these skills.

We are excited about the extended potential for Buyer Personas and are privileged to travel this path with the world's most amazing marketers. We can't wait to see where this takes all of us.

For now, start small and make a big difference.

Summary

In this chapter, we covered the following points:

- Start your Buyer Persona initiative with one well-defined project, goal, or campaign of interest – one that everyone agrees cannot be achieved by doing business as usual. Execute well and build on this initial success.
- Once you're perceived as a buyer expert, you have the opportunity to impact the entire business from acquisition to market expansion to product extensions and beyond.
- As you make discoveries about your buyer's needs, concerns, and expectations, focus on how marketing can contribute to these requirements before making demands from other functions that may need to play a role too (e.g. sales, customer service, product management).
- Look for ways to adapt the Buyer Persona methodology in other areas such as strategic planning, new product development, and forecasting.

Acknowledgments

I'd like to thank my family, Binita, Jessica, and Taylor, for their love and encouragement during the writing process, and our two dogs, Addie and Dakota, whose daily walks were always a welcomed break. Running a business and writing a book isn't for the faint at heart, but working on something that you're passionate about, that you can add value to, and that you believe will help others is a privilege that kept my engine running. I'm also grateful to have finally put my English degree to good use.

—Jim Kraus

I want to first thank my husband for suggesting, almost 25 years ago, that I pause my search for yet another VP role and consider what I really wanted to do next. I could never have imagined how that advice would lead to such intensely rewarding work. And then I must acknowledge my co-author Jim Kraus, who believed that merging our Buyer Persona methodology with KS&R's customer experience research would bring so much more value to our clients. I am simply blown away by how much Jim has improved upon everything I wanted to accomplish when I wrote the first edition of this book.

—Adele Revella

About the Authors

Jim Kraus is the President of Buyer Persona Institute (BPI), and a principal of Knowledge Systems & Research, Inc. (KS&R), a leading global market research and consulting firm. Jim has decades of experience leading research teams and developing growth strategies through informed decisions, including executive roles at both IBM and Prudential. A passionate advocate for the customer and accomplished speaker, Jim is known as a leading expert on buying decisions and the people who make them.

    Adele Revella is the CEO emeritus and Founder of Buyer Persona Institute (BPI). Adele is recognized for defining the Buyer Persona methodology that has become the gold standard for thousands of marketers in hundreds of global companies. She is widely recognized as a marketing and business leadership speaker, consultant, and author. In her distinguished career, Adele has seen the discipline from all sides: executive, consultant, trainer, and entrepreneur.

Index